One State, Many Nations

*Publication of this volume was made possible through
the Katrin H. Lamon Publications Fund at the School for Advanced Research.*

School for Advanced Research
Global Indigenous Politics Series

James F. Brooks
General Editor

One State, Many Nations
Indigenous Rights Struggles in Ecuador

Maximilian Viatori

SAR PRESS

School for Advanced Research Press
Santa Fe

School for Advanced Research Press
Post Office Box 2188
Santa Fe, New Mexico 87504-2188
www.sarpress.sarweb.org

Managing Editor: Lisa Pacheco
Editorial Assistant: Ellen Goldberg
Designer and Production Manager: Cynthia Dyer
Manuscript Editor: Kate Whelan
Proofreader: Amanda A. Morgan
Indexer: Catherine Fox
Printer: Transcontinental Printing

Library of Congress Cataloging-in-Publication Data

Viatori, Maximilian Stefan.
  One state, many nations : indigenous rights struggles in Ecuador / Maximilian Viatori.
      p. cm. — (School for Advanced Research global indigenous politics series)
  Includes bibliographical references and index.
  ISBN 978-1-934691-17-5 (alk. paper)
  1. Zaparo Indians—Civil rights—Ecuador. 2. Indigenous peoples—Civil rights—Ecuador.
  3. Civil rights movements—Ecuador. 4. Zaparo Indians—Ecuador—Politics and government.
  5. Zaparo Indians—Ecuador—Ethnic identity. 6. Zaparo language—Pollitical aspects—Ecuador.
  7. Zaparo Indians—Government policy—Ecuador. 8. Multiculturalism—Ecuador. 9. Ecuador—
  Ethnic relations. I. Title.
  F3722.1.Z3V53 2010
  323.1198'90866 229--dc'9

                            2009040768

Copyright © 2009 School for Advanced Research. All rights reserved.
Manufactured in Canada.
Library of Congress Catalog Card Number: 2009040768
International Standard Book Number 978-1-934691-17-5
First edition 2010.

This book was printed on 100% PCR

Cover illustration: Military exercise and onlooker in front of Ecuador's national capitol building, Ecuador. Photo by author.

For Mom and Dad

Contents

Figures

Acknowledgments

I owe my sincerest thanks to the Zápara nationality, its leaders and members, who opened their lives and homes to me. A number of other friends helped me out during my many stays in Ecuador: Casey and Mette High, Chris Krupa, Lara Iyer, the Morales family, and Jorge Gómez Rendón. My initial research was funded by grants and fellowships from the University of California, the Northern California chapter of Phi Beta Kappa, the Endangered Language Foundation, the Foundation for Endangered Languages, and the Wenner-Gren Foundation. The Department of Anthropology, the College of Liberal Arts and Sciences, and the Latin American Studies Program committee at Iowa State University paid for my return trips to Ecuador in the summers of 2006 and 2008.

As a graduate student at the University of California, Davis, I benefited from the assistance and attention of a number of faculty. I am especially thankful to Martha Macri, who was the most wonderful mentor and friend I could ask for. Of equal importance was the mentoring I received from Carol Smith, who helped me to articulate my research project and served as a key adviser after I graduated. Stefano Varese, Aram Yengoyan, Suzana Sawyer, and Janet Shibamoto-Smith also helped me at different points during my studies. I am grateful to my undergraduate mentor at the University of Missouri, N. Louanna Furbee, for sending me on my first trip to Latin America. Thanks to my colleagues in the anthropology department and in the American Indian studies and Latin American studies programs at Iowa State University for their support, especially Hsain Ilahiane for his constant encouragement and Grant Arndt and Dennis and Kate Kelley for the helpful conversations we had while I was revising this manuscript.

Marc Becker and an anonymous reviewer for SAR Press provided thoughtful, detailed feedback on how to improve an earlier version of the manuscript. Thanks also to Catherine Cocks for her interest in this project and help getting it published and to Kate Whelan for her meticulous work editing the final draft. An earlier version of chapter 2 was published in the *Journal of Latin American and Caribbean Anthropology* (12[1]:104–133). Brief portions of a research note that I authored in *Latin American and Caribbean Ethnic Studies* (3[2]:193–203) also appear in this book.

I am most grateful to my closest friends and family for their enduring support. Travis Hartman has been a constant source of inspiration and friendship and put up with me during a month in Puyo. Thanks to Chris and Susan MacMurdo for driving me to LAX airport in the middle of the night and for always being there. I am indebted to Hogan Martin for doing his best to get me away from my computer and keep me sane. Many thanks to the extended Mundel clan for their support. Thanks, also, to my grandparents for years of encouragement, and *tante grazie* to Gaga for our many afternoons of reading and talking. I cannot imagine completing this work without the support of my mother and father, as well as my brother, Ben, and sister, Melissa. My parents and siblings have done all they could to help me along. Thanks again for the phone calls, letters, unpaid loans, plane tickets, and understanding.

My greatest thanks go to Anneke Mundel, my amazing partner, who saw me through this project's numerous rough patches with unequaled kindness, love, and patience. And to my two magnificent boys, Elio and Nico, who infuse each of my days with joyful glee and a renewed appreciation for the small wonders of life. Words cannot express my gratitude.

1 Introduction

On the morning of May 20, 2001, I walked with a small group of friends along the Avenida Naciones Unidas in Quito, Ecuador (figure 1.1). We were on our way to see a movie at a theater that was a few blocks away. It was my first time outside in more than a week—I had been bedridden in a friend's apartment with a miserable combination of strep throat and malaria. As we made our way up the increasingly steep street, we stopped to wait for traffic at the intersection with 10 de Agosto, another of Quito's major thoroughfares. I was glad for the rest as my stamina had yet to return and it gave me a minute to enjoy the warming effect of the equatorial sun. We bought a copy of *El Comercio*, Ecuador's largest daily newspaper, from a corner vendor to check movie times. I immediately forgot about the movie listings when I saw an article on the front page announcing that the United Nations Educational, Scientific and Cultural Organization (UNESCO) had declared the Zápara "ethnicity" part of the "Intangible and Oral Patrimony of Humankind." The article explained that the Zápara were a small Indigenous group in Ecuador's Amazonian rain forest whose language was spoken by fewer than five elders and in danger of extinction as a result of the harms of "modernity, technological development and globalization" (*El Comercio* 2001). Another paper quoted an Ecuadorian anthropologist who said, "We should feel proud of our roots" because the Zápara are a national treasure (*El Universo* 2001).

Zápara is a member of the Zaparoan language family, a small group of Amazonian languages in eastern Ecuador and northern Peru, all of which are now dead or highly endangered (Peeke 1962, 1991; Stark 1981:12–13; Wise 1999:312). On May 18 UNESCO pledged to aid the Zápara in preserving their language and oral tradition.

In March 2001 I went to Ecuador to help document the Zápara language. The Zápara are one of the smallest Indigenous nationalities in Ecuador, with

Figure 1.1 Avenida Naciones Unidas in Quito. Photo by author.

roughly two hundred members, most of whom live along the Conambo and Pindoyacu rivers in Pastaza province. The Zápara were decimated during the rubber boom that swept through the Upper Amazon basin at the end of the nineteenth century. As a result of epidemics and forced labor at the hands of rubber merchants, the Zápara, like many other Indigenous peoples in the region, experienced a dramatic population decline during the late nineteenth and early twentieth centuries. Following the rubber boom, most of the remaining Zápara were assimilated by their Kichwa neighbors.[1] In 1998 four communities—Llanchamacocha, Jandiayacu, Mazaramu, and Cuyacocha—organized as the Nacionalidad Zápara de Ecuador (Zápara Nationality of Ecuador, NAZAE) with the intent of reasserting Zápara identity and establishing a legal Zápara territory distinct from those of other Indigenous nationalities in the region (figure 1.2). At the heart of this revitalization was an attempt to document the language of the remaining Zápara elders as proof of these communities' cultural uniqueness.

While I was sick in Quito, I forgot that UNESCO was due to announce its list of candidates for its Intangible Cultural Heritage project. I found a phone booth near the movie theater and called to congratulate a colleague who had worked on the project. Later that day, one of Ecuador's television stations ran a segment on the Zápara, including comments by an

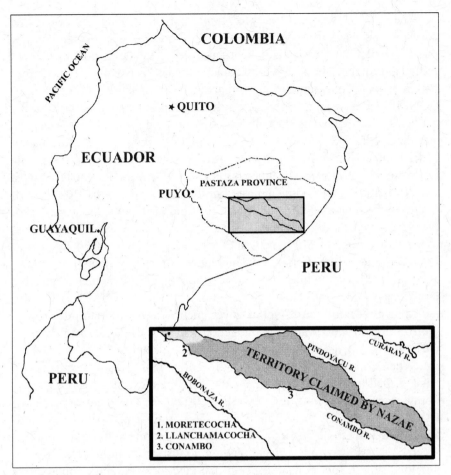

Figure 1.2 Geographic location of the Zápara nationality in Ecuador. Adapted from NAZAE's Mapa del territorio (2003).

Ecuadorian linguist and a Zápara leader on the importance of the language for the perpetuation of Zápara cultural identity. UNESCO's recognition was a boon for NAZAE and its efforts at revival—shortly afterwards, the Ecuadorian government followed suit by publicly recognizing the Zápara. In May 2001 Ecuador's congress celebrated the Záparas' UNESCO award, and Ecuador's Ministerio de Educación, Cultura, Deportes y Recreación (Ministry of Education, Culture, Sports and Recreation, or MEC) bestowed the Medal of Cultural Merit of the First Class on the Zápara people. MEC's Ministerial Accord No. 552 recognized the Zápara for their "rich cultural tradition," expressed in their language, and their determination to save this component of Ecuador's "national cultural patrimony" from disappearance.

The Záparas' warm official reception stood in striking contrast to the government's reaction to Indigenous protests and political demands a few months earlier. In January and February 2001, Ecuador's most prominent Indigenous organization, the Confederación de las Nacionalidades Indígenas del Ecuador (Confederation of Indigenous Nationalities of Ecuador, or CONAIE) led a national mobilization demanding government action for the country's poor. Following the collapse of its banking system in 1999 and the adoption of the US dollar as its currency in 2000, Ecuador suffered inflation and heightened unemployment. CONAIE's protest was aimed at decreasing the price of transportation and stopping tax increases on public services (CONAIE 2001). In response, interim president Gustavo Noboa (2000–2003) deployed the military and police to halt the demonstrations. Indigenous people were forced from buses and detained, and protestors were denied access to their usual camp in Quito's central El Arbolito park (Macdonald 2002:188). Press coverage of the mobilization highlighted "the government's repressive and violent acts" while generally supporting Indigenous protestors (Macdonald 2002:188). However, as the year moved on and CONAIE maintained its opposition to the Noboa government, the Ecuadorian press took a more critical stance towards the Indigenous confederation, focusing on internal conflicts and alleged corruption within its leadership.

When compared, these two instances highlight a distinction between what Ecuadorian elites viewed as the "acceptable" and "inappropriate" boundaries of Indigenous identity (Hale 2002:507). Government representatives celebrated Zápara "ethnicity" as an important aspect of Ecuador's cultural past, something to be preserved for future generations. In contrast, when CONAIE demanded greater economic justice for Indigenous peoples and inclusion in government decision-making processes, elites opposed this expression of Indigenous ethnicity as a divisive force in national politics. What emerges from this scenario is a paradox: according to powerful actors and institutions, Indigenous identity is good in some cases but bad in others (Hale 2002:493, 2004:17; see also Gustafson 2002). Ethnicity is acceptable when it involves expressions of cultural difference such as clothing, dance, and music (Tilley 2002:536). However, it is objectionable when Indigenous peoples agitate for concrete improvements in their economic and political situations (Postero 2007:15).

Indigenous Rights in Neoliberal Times

The paradoxical treatment of Indigenous identity is the subject of this book. My purpose is to explore the official recognition of ethnic and cultural difference in Ecuador with the following question in mind: has the official recognition of Indigenous rights provided new opportunities for Indigenous actors or further restricted their political action?

Ecuador has been at the vanguard of Latin America's Indigenous rights reforms. In 1998 the country's constitution was revised to give Indigenous peoples expanded linguistic, cultural, and territorial rights—what political scientist Donna Lee Van Cott (2005:126) believes was the "most progressive" package of Indigenous constitutional rights at the time. In 2008 Ecuador's new constitution declared the country a plurinational state. As Ecuadorian governments instituted some of their most extensive reforms, a host of other Latin American states with Indigenous populations, such as Colombia, Guatemala, and Bolivia, made similar constitutional modifications (Yashar 2005).

The question of how to interpret these reforms is one of the central topics in current studies of Latin American nation-states and Indigenous peoples. Anthropologists and other social scientists debate why these reforms have emerged in recent decades. I use the phrase *official multiculturalism* throughout this chapter to refer to elite-sponsored reforms that are concerned primarily with recognizing ethnic diversity, in contrast to Indigenous notions of *interculturalism* and *plurinationality*, which stress the need for more substantive economic and political rights.[2] A number of authors have argued that multicultural reforms are the result of powerful Indigenous movements pressuring traditional elites—weakened by economic crises and the return to formal democracy in much of Latin America—to accept more inclusive notions of citizenship.[3]

However, anthropologist Charles Hale (2002, 2005) has questioned the notion that Indigenous people were able to force ethnic reforms on reluctant states. Based on his own ethnographic research in Central America, Hale argues that official multicultural reforms represent an attempt by national and international elites to redefine citizenship and political participation by adopting a limited package of Indigenous rights that reinforces current forms of social, political, and economic dominance. Hale (2004) argues that Indigenous leaders and communities who stick to these "permitted" rights receive state recognition and resources (see also Rivera Cusicanqui 2008:143). However, those who choose to push for "unacceptable" rights, which contest existing political economies and social structures—such as the redistribution of concrete resources—are relegated to the political and economic margins (Hale 2002:491). The result is a deepening "division among different strands of cultural rights activism" that poses a greater "menace" to Indigenous movements than did previous doctrines of assimilation (Hale 2002:485, 491).

Anthropologists Shannon Speed and Nancy Grey Postero have contested

Hale's vision of official multiculturalism. They argue that although official discourses of Indigenous recognition have renewed prior histories of racial discrimination and ethnic marginalization, these have also created new spaces for Indigenous activism that contest dominant paradigms of exclusion. In southern Mexico, Speed (2006a) argues, Zapatista communities have avoided the traps of official multiculturalism by constructing their autonomy outside the legal frameworks of the state and developing a more expansive set of Indigenous rights than those advocated by government elites. In Postero's (2007:16) work on Bolivia, she suggests that Indigenous activists used the spaces created by multicultural reforms to question the very foundation upon which these reforms were built and to "push beyond" their limitations. The result, she argues, has been the emergence of a "post-multicultural" citizenship in Bolivia—Indigenous activists have created alliances with other sectors of society to fight for access to political power as Bolivian citizens, rather than demand greater rights based on their ethnic and racial difference (Postero 2007:18).

The core issue of this debate is whether multicultural reforms have stood in opposition to or have been seamlessly integrated into larger economic and political changes made by many Latin American states to improve their positions in the global marketplace. The 1980s and 1990s were decades of economic turmoil and political change throughout much of Latin America. Spurred by the 1982 worldwide economic crisis, countries in the region plunged into debt as international commodity prices fell and interest rates soared. As a result, most of Latin America's national governments were forced to take out expansive loans from the International Monetary Fund (IMF) and the World Bank. These institutions not only provided financing at inflated repayment rates but also required that debtor states undertake neoliberal economic, political, and social reforms. *Neoliberalism* refers to the ideology that the most effective means for maximizing social good is to liberate "individual entrepreneurial freedoms and skills within an institutional framework characterized by strong private property rights, free markets and free trade" (Harvey 2005:2; see also Ferguson 2006). In Latin America, neoliberalism has been characterized by a broad set of policies that have included governmental decentralization, privatization of state resources, decreased economic regulations, and cuts in social spending. These policies are aimed at decreasing government interference in the free market—except where military and legal means are necessary "to secure private property rights and to guarantee, by force if need be, the proper functioning of markets" (Harvey 2005:2).

In Ecuador, neoliberal reform has "been implemented in a less orthodox fashion and at a slower pace" than in other Latin American states (Lind

2005:62), such as Bolivia, which underwent perhaps the harshest economic adjustment in the region (see Gill 2000). Nevertheless, Ecuador's neoliberal policies have had a profound "effect on the organization of the economy, the state, and civil society" (Lind 2005:62). Beginning in the 1980s, Ecuador's governments introduced economic austerity measures to offset a domestic economic crisis caused by a plummet in international oil prices and a jump in interest rates. In 1971, service to foreign debts accounted for $15 of every $100 exported—by 1981, the ratio had grown to $71 for every $100 exported (Acosta 2003:79–80). Between 1982 and 1988, per capita income in Ecuador fell by 32 percent, and the country's foreign debt climbed from 37 percent to 122 percent of its Gross Domestic Product (GDP) (Treakle 1998:222). However, neoliberal adjustment proceeded in a start-and-stop manner throughout the 1980s because the general populace resisted cuts in government spending and some government elites opposed limiting state control of the national economy (see Sawyer 2004:11–15). It was not until the 1990s, when Ecuador's financial crisis worsened, that the country's governments pursued more severe economic austerity policies. Throughout much of the 1990s, Ecuador claimed the "highest per capita foreign debt...in Latin America" (Sawyer 2004:95). In response to Ecuador's fiscal crisis, the Durán Ballén administration (1992–1996) instituted the first comprehensive neoliberal reform package in Ecuador: dismantling tariff protections, deregulating domestic markets, eliminating subsidies, and partially deregulating the financing system (see Larrea and Sánchez 2003:8; Lind 2004:62; Sawyer 2004:11). Durán Ballén also withdrew Ecuador from the Organization of Petroleum Exporting Countries (OPEC) in 1992 so that it could "produce in excess of the country's production quota," increasing its output of petroleum by almost one hundred thousand barrels per day (Sawyer 2004:95).

Rather than improve, Ecuador's economy deteriorated as the international price of oil declined. Between November 1998 and 1999, Ecuador's banking system collapsed. President Jamil Mahuad (1998–2000) attempted to bail out Ecuador's five main banks but was not able to resuscitate the failing institutions (Macdonald 2002:171). The value of Ecuador's national currency, the sucre, plummeted, and the country's GDP dropped more than 6 percent in 1999. As a sign of its deepening troubles, Ecuador defaulted on payment of its $6 billion Brady Bond debt, further tarnishing its already battered reputation in the international financial markets. The country was at the mercy of the IMF and World Bank, which controlled 85 percent of its foreign loans and therefore "profoundly influenced policies, projects, and in many cases legislation in the country" (Treakle 1998:224).[4] The IMF advised the Ecuadorian government to raise prices and cut expenditures. Between

1995 and 2001, government spending on education dropped from 63 percent of all social spending in the national budget to 46 percent, and spending on health care declined from 22 percent to 15 percent (Parandekar, Vos, and Winkler 2002:149). In 2001 the Ecuadorian government paid $1.6 billion towards its foreign debts—more than double the amount it spent on education, health, and internal development combined (CAAP 2003:12).

This reduction in the scope of state social expenditures has led to what sociologist Leon Zamosc (2004) describes as a combined crisis of representation and state legitimacy. He argues that this "dual political crisis" resulted from the fact that neoliberal adjustments worsened Ecuador's economic situation, causing a decline in the state's authority because many Ecuadorians viewed their government as "ineffective and grossly unjust" (Zamosc 2004: 140, 151). This was exacerbated by the government's weakened ability to provide for the well-being of its citizens and by Ecuador's traditional political elites' disregard for the impact of neoliberalism on the general populace (Zamosc 2004:143).

Anthropologist Suzana Sawyer (2004:15) asserts that the weakened credibility of Ecuador's state system opened political space for the development of a radical Indigenous movement in the gap that neoliberalism created between the state and its citizenry. Sawyer (2004:15) argues that while neoliberalism increased the economic marginalization of Indigenous peoples in Ecuador, it also created "the conditions of possibility for a disruptive indigenous movement that denounced the government's allegiances to transnational capital and its unresponsiveness to subaltern subjects." For instance, the decentralization of traditional state responsibilities has been an important factor in establishing the political legitimacy of Ecuador's Indigenous organizations, many of whom took over the administration of community social services from the state in the 1980s (see Crain 1990:48–49; Zamosc 1994:54). According to Sawyer, Indigenous organizations used this legitimacy to highlight the economic ills of neoliberalism. Moreover, they rejected the idea of official multiculturalism, advocating for intercultural cooperation and the acknowledgment that Ecuador was plurinational—a state consisting of multiple nationalities with equal rights in government, society, and the economy. Utilizing the concept of plurinationalism, Sawyer (2004:10) argues that Indigenous organizations reconfigured the way in which citizens conceptualized the Ecuadorian nation-state.

Building on Sawyer's analysis, I show that official multicultural reforms have generated novel openings for Indigenous organizations. However, I argue that these reforms have simultaneously limited the parameters of Indigenous activism and produced new divisions in local movements.

Despite being riddled with "internal conflicts" (Striffler 2002:37–38), the Ecuadorian state's "regulative and coercive" agencies have the ability to define "certain kinds of subjects and identities" while "ruling out" others (Roseberry 1994:355). Notwithstanding declines in state corporatist projects and funding for social welfare throughout Latin America, Indigenous organizations must register with the "right ministry, in accordance with the appropriate law," work with traditional political parties to evoke constitutional changes, and petition government bureaus for land titles (Lucero 2003:41; see also Hodgson 2002:1041).

Moreover, the state is not the only powerful actor involved in articulating spaces of Indigenous recognition and participation in Ecuador. Although state spending for Indigenous education and social welfare has slowed to a trickle, the World Bank, the United Nations, and a multitude of NGOs have increased funding for Indigenous development, education, and environmental preservation projects. These state-like actors represent a significant source of human and financial capital for resource-poor Indigenous communities, especially in Ecuador's Amazonian region—where the state historically has been absent from daily social life. As such, these state-like actors have the ability to shape Indigenous political participation by providing grants and training to organizations and community projects that fit their own financial, social, or political agendas. For example, World Bank staffers chose not to work directly with CONAIE and other national-level organizations when sponsoring a new "ethno-development" project in Ecuador (the subject of this book's penultimate chapter), claiming that such organizations were too "politically motivated" and not responsive to local needs (Van Nieuwkoop and Uquillas 2000:12).

The result has been that official multicultural reforms have made it more difficult for Indigenous organizations to effect radical change. Ecuadorian scholar José Almeida Vinueza (2005:93) argues that the Ecuadorian state, multinational lenders, and donor agencies have successfully "appropriated" the Indigenous movement's concepts of interculturalism and plurinationalism, altering their meanings and stripping them of their potential for evoking more expansive notions of social change. As Almeida Vinueza (2005: 93,104) suggests, dominant policies of multiculturalism have emphasized tangible aspects of local "cultures" over pan-Indigenous political identities, free-market initiatives over resource redistribution, and applications for development projects over collective political action. This has not spelled the end of Indigenous activism in Ecuador, but, as this book demonstrates, it has erected significant barriers for Indigenous federations pushing for far-reaching change and local communities seeking greater autonomy.

National Reforms, Local Concerns

A number of excellent studies on Indigenous politics in Ecuador exist. However, most have focused on Indigenous activism and Indigenous–state relationships at the national level.[5] Although these studies have mapped out the major issues at play in Ecuador's ethnic politics, they have overlooked the effects of these politics on local organizations (Lucero 2006a:32–33). The significance of Ecuador's official multiculturalism for Indigenous peoples' day-to-day lives has remained largely unexplored, despite the fact that such information is critical for assessing the full impact of these reforms.

Given this gap in the literature, I chose to ground my analysis of official multiculturalism in an ethnographic study of the Zápara nationality, the group mentioned at the beginning of this chapter. This book traces the Zápara nationality's process of self-organization and emergence within Ecuador's Indigenous movement from 1998 to 2008, to explore the complex role that multiculturalism has played in local Indigenous politics.

The Zápara provide an important perspective on official multiculturalism for a number of reasons. They were one of many grassroots Indigenous organizations to emerge at the time of Ecuador's 1998 constitutional reforms. As political scientist Victor Bretón (2005:72) notes, the majority of these organizations were not able to take full advantage of emerging national reforms to solidify their organizational bases. In contrast, NAZAE appeared to exploit the openings created by official multicultural reforms in a manner incomparable to other grassroots Indigenous organizations. In the space of five years, the organization gained administrative control and government funding for education in its communities, obtained thousands of dollars from the World Bank, secured multiyear funding from UNESCO for language documentation, and received a host of smaller grants from environmental NGOs for ecological protection. For a new and relatively small organization, NAZAE was able to position itself effectively within regional, national, and international rights networks—providing what seemed to be an example of the opportunities created by official multicultural reforms for local organizations.

However, while official multicultural reforms opened new spaces for the assertion of Zápara political subjectivity in Ecuador, they also expanded and naturalized dominant understandings of Indigenous identity and political participation in NAZAE. Zápara leaders were able to draw tens of thousands of dollars from powerful supporters, but they did so by fashioning a version of local identity that fit elite spaces of recognition—one that dismissed important aspects of Zápara history, practice, and pan-community cooperation. Moreover, despite official multiculturalism's initial promise of expanded autonomy for Indigenous organizations and their communities,

NAZAE increasingly found itself dependent on outside "experts." Dominant institutions' emphases on narrowly defined projects not only devalued the knowledge accrued by NAZAE leaders in community mobilization and collective activism but also stressed the importance of formal education and technical knowledge that these leaders did not yet possess.

Finally, official multiculturalism's emphasis on local differences as the legitimate indicators of Indigenous identity—variations in dress, language, and economic production—led to bitter disputes within the Zápara nationality over which groups or families were most entitled to recognition and funding. Although NAZAE has consistently represented the majority of Zápara in Ecuador, another organization—which I refer to throughout the book as the Comuna Záparo (Záparo Commune)—has claimed Zápara identity since the mid-1990s (an issue I discuss in chapter 3). Over the past decade, the two organizations have fought each other through various government ministries, each petitioning at different points to have the other's official status revoked. This is an unfortunate trend that has been mirrored in recent years at regional and national levels as state officials have actively sought to exploit rifts within Ecuador's national Indigenous movement.

Although the Zápara are one of Ecuador's smallest nationalities, their organization's trajectory has paralleled important developments in official reform and Indigenous activism in Ecuador. This book is not only an in-depth ethnographic account of the diverse political actions in which NAZAE leaders have been engaged, but also a view of the broader problems and conflicts that Ecuador's Indigenous organizations face. Each of the book's chapters elucidates a different aspect of official multiculturalism in Ecuador and its role in constructing local Indigenous identities.

Chapter 2 provides the historical background for the Záparas' emergence in Ecuadorian Indigenous politics. It outlines the ways in which Zápara practice and identity have been shaped through the nationality's links to regional, national, and global political economies. Moreover, it shows that official multicultural reforms are the latest in a series of attempts by elite actors to shape Indigenous identities to fit Ecuador's changing social landscape. Chapter 3 examines NAZAE's entrance into Indigenous politics and reveals the complex manner in which Zápara leaders adapted their communities' history and cultural practices—particularly in their use of language to symbolize cultural legitimacy—to fit emergent multicultural and plurinational paradigms. It also shows that, in the process of reshaping Zápara identity to fit new multicultural frameworks, these leaders reinforced dominant and often stereotypical understandings of Indigenous identity in their communities and in their relations with rival Zápara leaders.

Chapters 4 through 6 examine the role of official multiculturalism in creating space for Zápara activism and simultaneously reinforcing restricted parameters of identity and practice. Chapter 4 explores the difficulties of implementing bilingual, intercultural education in local Zápara schools. Although administrative control of local education augmented NAZAE's organizational capacities, government spending cuts precluded significant improvements in Zápara community education. Chapter 5 probes the function of sympathetic non-Indigenous advocates and their work with NAZAE leaders on UNESCO's project to document the Zápara language. It demonstrates that such advocacy has been essential for NAZAE's ability to exploit international discourses of Indigenous rights but has also produced relationships of dependency between Indigenous activists and their non-Indigenous counterparts. Chapter 6 looks at a World Bank–funded project aimed at mitigating Indigenous peoples' economic marginalization by augmenting their "social capital." Rather than enhance Zápara political and economic autonomy, I argue, this project reinforced a narrow (and decidedly apolitical) version of what "counted" as Zápara identity, encouraging a dependent relationship between NAZAE and the project apparatus.

In the book's final chapter, I discuss NAZAE's decline after a steady rise to prominence within regional Indigenous politics. I argue that, despite initial efforts to take advantage of the openings created by recent official multicultural discourses in Ecuador, the contradictory aspects of these reforms have made it difficult for the Zápara to sustain their political activism. I then discuss the ways in which the Záparas' situation has paralleled that of other Indigenous nationalities in Ecuador and the current situation of Indigenous activism in the country.

Studying Indigenous Activism

My book's analysis is rooted in more than a year of ethnographic research conducted during five visits to Ecuador between 2001 and 2004, with follow-up visits in 2006 and 2008. I spent most of these visits as a participant-observer in NAZAE, studying Zápara activism by being involved in it. I shadowed NAZAE activists during their day-to-day activities, observing their interactions with other Indigenous leaders, government officials, non-Indigenous volunteers, and NGO workers. I accompanied them on four trips, lasting from a few days to a month, to Zápara communities along the Conambo River (and once to meet a Zápara speaker on the Curaray River). During these trips, I observed Zápara leaders' interactions with their constituents and talked to community residents on their own. I conversed with Zápara-speaking elders, recorded linguistic information about Zápara, collected oral histories, and discussed identity and politics with younger Zápara. Furthermore, I studied the "paper trail"—memos, legal documents, and proposals—that detailed NAZAE's interactions with various state agencies and non-state institutions. I spoke with officials in relevant ministries and members of other Indigenous federations in Pastaza. Finally, I examined press releases and media interviews with Zápara leaders that documented their strategies for representing Zápara identity.

I intentionally submerged myself in NAZAE's daily activities as a means to study the dynamics of the organization and the processes through which Zápara identity and political participation were constructed.[6] In contrast to a broader comparative approach, focusing exclusively on NAZAE enabled me to examine the intricate spaces where local understandings of national identity and political inclusion took shape (Canessa 2005:6, 18). The compromise of this approach was that the resulting study represents an examination of Indigenous organizing from a relatively narrow, local perspective.

Furthermore, my research was driven and informed by my ongoing cooperation with NAZAE on the documentation of the language. Zápara leaders were cautious about working with social scientists, especially because Ecuadorian anthropologists had declared the Zápara "extinct" (Andrade Pallares 2001:20; Costales and Costales Samaniego 1975). My basic linguistic training was welcomed by NAZAE in its efforts to revive the Zápara language—I recorded Zápara narratives, worked on bilingual Zápara–Spanish pedagogical materials, and applied for (and received) grant money to carry out these small projects. I began my linguistic work with the Zápara as a project aimed at helping Indigenous communities to revalorize an endangered language. This soon morphed into an effort to help the Zápara document their language and oral history as a means for establishing government recognition and territorial rights.

My linguistic work positioned me as an advocate of the Záparas' struggle and underpinned my ethnographic research within NAZAE. To understand the micropolitics of Indigenous organization, language use and identity, and cultural rights, I spent countless hours conversing, traveling, living, working, joking, and eating with NAZAE leaders. Such constant and close interaction with my research participants required a level of trust that my cooperative work granted me (Sawyer 2004:22). The result was that my research was situated in the tense middle ground between "activist research"—aligning oneself with a group of people and their struggle and using one's academic authority to aid in their rights claims—and "cultural critique"—intellectual analysis of the complexities and contradictions of dominant and subaltern politics, uncompromised by the negotiations of on-the-ground struggles (Hale 2006:97–98; see also Speed 2006b).

To balance the narrow scope and subjective character of my study, throughout this book I situate NAZAE's activities within larger processes at work not only in Ecuador's Indigenous movement but also in Ecuadorian politics and transnational economics. Each chapter reveals how the dynamics at work within NAZAE often paralleled those of CONAIE and other Indigenous nationalities, and the significance of divergences between NAZAE's situation and those of other Indigenous peoples. Thus, this study examines CONAIE from the perspective of one of its small member organizations, providing a detailed local account of one of the hemisphere's most renowned social movements.

Names and Terms

I use pseudonyms to refer to most of the people who appear in this book—Zápara activists and their constituents, Zápara elders, and NGO workers. In several instances, I modified key aspects of individuals' life histories when I thought that a pseudonym was not sufficient to disguise their identities. However, I use the real names of Indigenous leaders such as NAZAE's president because they occupied prominent public roles.[7] It would have been impossible to hide their identities and would have likely caused confusion for those acquainted with Ecuadorian Indigenous politics.

Within anthropology and Indigenous studies, there has been an ongoing debate about the terms used to refer to Indigenous peoples. There is no standardized term that is universally agreed upon by Indigenous peoples and scholars throughout the Americas, because different signifiers have different connotations in different countries (Warren and Jackson 2002:29). In Ecuador, Indigenous peoples have preferred to call themselves *Indígenas* over the somewhat pejorative *Indio* (Indian). For this reason, I have chosen not to use *Indian* in this book. Yet, there is no direct cognate of *Indígena* in English. The closest approximation would be *Indigene*, which is "not really English" (Warren and Jackson 2002:29). I finally decided on the term *Indigenous peoples*, capitalizing *Indigenous* throughout to retain its proper status in English. Although the word *peoples* has been contested by some academics because of its relationship to nineteenth-century European concepts of nationhood, it has been adopted by a number of Indigenous activists and scholars as an acceptable and, for some, even desirable term (see Holm, Pearson, and Chasis 2003).

2 Language, History, and Zápara Identity

In August 2002 I traveled down the Conambo River from Llanchamacocha to Jandiayacu to contact Carlos, one of the few remaining Zápara speakers. I went with María, a NAZAE *dirigente* (leader), and several of Carlos's relatives from Llanchamacocha. The trip took us two days as we meandered along the snaking Conambo (figure 2.1) in a long, thin dugout canoe with a leaky bow. The river had recently crested and the water was low. Downed trees seemed to block our passage at every turn. On the first day, we stopped frequently to push and pull the heavy canoe over low-lying barriers—at times, we chopped through larger, higher tree trunks. Despite the extra work, the journey was enjoyable. As the lush trees of the rain forest passed by at the pace of the slow-moving water, we talked, told stories, and listened for howler monkeys and birds. From time to time, we stopped on a bank to drink sweet banana *chicha* (beer) that María's mother—one of Carlos's sisters—had made in the days before we left. When evening approached, we set up camp on a sandy beach and watched the sun set over the tops of the trees.

Although Jandiayacu straddles the Conambo, most of the community is concentrated on the northeast side of the river—around the airstrip, the school, and Carlos's spacious house. We began our visit by mooring the canoe on the southwest bank in front of the house of Fernando, one of Carlos's sons, where we drank chicha and made sleeping arrangements. Then we crossed the narrow river in another canoe, piloted by Fernando's son, and made our way along a slippery path to Carlos's house, where we were welcomed with more chicha (figure 2.2). The Zápara elder was an affable host and an animated storyteller; he fit the role of community patriarch well. His back was bent slightly from years of manual labor, and one of his eyes showed the telltale clouding of a cataract.

Figure 2.1 The Conambo River. Photo by author.

Over the course of the next few weeks, Carlos became my guide through Zápara history and my instructor in the language. Most days, Carlos and I met and talked in the mornings and then again in the afternoons after he had eaten and rested. Sometimes, María and others were present for our conversations; other times, it was just the two of us. Carlos gave me lessons in Zápara, like the ones he gave several times a week to the community's students, many of whom were his grandchildren. He taught greetings, vocabulary, and short phrases in the language. The remainder of the time, Carlos recounted lengthy stories about the origins of the Zápara people, their migrations, and their fights with other groups. He would then turn to accounts of more recent history—one scarred by violent change and destruction. Carlos told me stories about the hard times his family encountered during the Amazon's rubber boom in the late nineteenth and early twentieth centuries, the border war between Peru and Ecuador in 1941, and the advent of oil extraction during the mid-twentieth century. All these factors, he would remind me, led to the demise of the Zápara as neighboring Indigenous groups increasingly assimilated them.

Carlos often struck me as an emblem of the changes the Zápara had undergone—a product of the social upheaval of the past century and the linguistic and cultural hybridity that ensued in its aftermath. His parents

Figure 2.2 Zápara men drinking chicha and making music in the community of Jandiayacu. Photo by author.

were Zápara speakers who engaged in subsistence hunting and swidden agriculture. Also, like many other Zápara of their generation, they had worked (freely or otherwise) as rubber tappers to obtain salt, clothes, and machetes. Carlos learned to speak Zápara from his parents but at a young age also learned Kichwa—his primary language—from relatives and community members. As a young man, he learned Spanish while working for Shell Oil Company. Before returning to his community, he spent a number of years working in Puyo and in the Sierra. Carlos's multilingualism was evident in his historical narratives. When he talked about mythological times, he would try telling the histories in Zápara, often with Kichwa mixed in, asking me to record him with my small digital player. Usually, he would say that he was too old or too sick (one time showing me a disturbingly large tumor on his back) to speak in Zápara, because of the effort it required. When this happened, he would tell more recent histories in Spanish or Kichwa or a mix of the two.

This chapter chronicles the tumultuous nature of the Záparas' interactions with white-mestizo elites and the role that these interactions played in profoundly reshaping Zápara language use and identity. Current narratives of Indigeneity often situate Amazonian peoples as developing autochthonous cultural identities outside the realm of modern capitalist society—a sentiment that has been echoed in ethnographies about Amazonian peoples. During the 1970s and 1980s, post-colonial and post-modern theorists questioned anthropology's approach to studying culture as a locally circumscribed, ahistorical process. In response, most ethnographers shifted their focus to the ways in which local manifestations of culture were linked to regional, national, and global political economies. However, anthropologist Steven Rubenstein (2007:358) argues that Amazonian specialists continued to emphasize the local qualities of social and economic relations within Indigenous communities. This resulted in what Rubenstein (2007:358) deems a renewed "bifurcation" in anthropology's approach to different research subjects, one that reinforces the division between "savagery" and "civilization" by situating Amazonian peoples firmly outside the realm of global history and transnational relations.[1] One consequence of this has been that anthropological studies of Amazonian peoples have often overlooked the conditions under which seemingly static practices, identities, and social meanings emerged or were altered by changes in the broader socioeconomic contexts in which they were situated.

Following Rubenstein's admonition for more inclusive Amazonian ethnography, I provide a history of Zápara identity and language use that demonstrates how the two have been linked to broader political economies. Rather than emphasize the apparent isolation, remoteness, or internal cohesion of Zápara communities, my purpose here is, as anthropologist Orin Starn (1999:21) puts it, "to explore what it would mean to understand culture and identity as a result of the continuous interplay between the village, the region, and the world." To paraphrase Starn (1999:21), Zápara understandings of themselves and the world have been connected to regional and transnational processes since the arrival of European explorers and missionaries. Over the past century, these links have become stronger as the Amazon has been further integrated into Ecuador's national imaginary and the world economy. I pay particular attention to the different meanings that have been attached to the Zápara language as an emblem of local identity—from marking people in the nineteenth century as "good" or "bad" for particular kinds of labor, to symbolizing communities in need of "saving" from the onslaught of twentieth-century globalization. I conclude this chapter by arguing that an awareness of these changes is crucial for understanding the challenges contemporary Zápara face as they attempt to fashion continuity in their language use and practice out of a history of shifting cultural meanings and social forms.

Contact, Missionaries, and Traders

Throughout most of Ecuador's colonial and post-colonial history, elites perceived the Amazon as an inhospitable land populated by "savages" who were ill suited to agricultural labor (Radcliffe and Westwood 1996:110). For the most part, the state left governance of the region to missionaries, traders, and the odd administrator banished to the Amazonian hinterlands. The Amazon, often referred to as the *Oriente* or the East, had a long period of isolation from elite centers and neglect by Ecuadorian governments, and Amazonian peoples have had a "very different relationship to the state than have highland groups" (Erazo 2007:179). The vast majority of highland Indigenous peoples were incorporated into Ecuador's extensive hacienda system as *peones* (serfs) who were literally tied to the land on which they worked. As such, relatively few autonomous Indigenous communities survived in the Ecuadorian Andes (Clark 2005:56; Clark and Becker 2007:3).[2] Amazonian groups were able to maintain greater cultural, linguistic, and political autonomy because of their more sporadic contact with dominant actors and institutions (Yashar 2005:111). Nonetheless, a number of state-like agents—particularly missionaries, traders, and, later, oil companies—have played a significant role in attempting to shape Indigenous identities and practice to fit the demands of regional political economies.

In 1541 Gonzalo Pizarro set out east of the Ecuadorian Andes to find the fabled city of El Dorado. His expedition was largely unsuccessful—he returned to Quito with only a fraction of his original company and no gold to speak of. However, a small band of Pizarro's men led by Francisco Orellana, who had split from the larger group, successfully descended the full length of the Amazon in a much-mythologized journey, encountering vast kingdoms and female warriors and declaring the region the property of the Spanish Empire (figure 2.3) (Carvajal 1934; Slater 2004:86–94). Shortly afterward, in the 1550s and 1560s, Spanish conquistadors and priests followed and established outposts that became administrative centers of the Spanish Empire in the Ecuadorian Amazon. The Spanish awarded *encomiendas* (royal estates) to loyal soldiers, who were allowed to collect tribute from the Indigenous people living within their estates or enlist them in collecting forest products such as gold, fibers, and resin (Muratorio 1991:2; A.-C. Taylor 1999:215). In addition to the encomiendas, the Spanish sought to control the region's inhabitants by constructing mission *reducciones* (settlements), where Jesuit priests tried to pacify and indoctrinate Indigenous peoples.

Yet, Spanish attempts at domination were "not easily accomplished" (Muratorio 1991:2), although they did leave a profound mark on the Western Amazon's social makeup. The greatest blight was the diseases that

Figure 2.3 A placard near the national capitol in Quito reads "The Discovery of the Amazon River Is the Glory of Quito." Photo by author.

swept through the epidemic-prone missions (Cleary 2001:87–88). As anthropologist Anne-Christine Taylor notes:

> The terrible mortality and the consequent disintegration of the social fabric of that part of the Amazon was largely due to the presence of numerous and relatively concentrated centers—either reductions or colonial establishments—for the propagation of infectious diseases, connected by the dense communications network linking the Jesuit missions with each other and to Spanish-mestizo poles of settlement. Epidemics thus spread very rapidly and over great distances. Throughout the seventeenth century they surged across the region roughly every 20 years, or every generation. Then, after a relative lull between 1690 and 1750, the process accelerated once again.... The decade 1750–1760 probably marked the absolute demographic nadir in the central and northern upper Amazon region. (1999:238–239)

In addition to declining populations of Indigenous laborers as a result of disease, Spanish reducciones and encomiendas were troubled by active and passive resistance on the part of Indigenous peoples. Indigenous revolts disrupted the construction and functioning of Jesuit, Franciscan, and Dominican missions in the Ecuadorian and Peruvian Amazon. Anthropologist Stefano Varese (2002:82–109) calls the 1700s a "century of rebellion" in the Peruvian Amazon, because Indigenous peoples such as the Ashaninka staged numerous armed uprisings against Spanish priests and settlers. In the southern Ecuadorian Amazon, the Shuar successfully fought off Spanish encroachment, developing a reputation as a particularly bellicose people as a result of their fabled 1599 uprising against the governor of Macas and gold miners in the region (Harner 1972:18–25). In addition to staging active rebellions, Indigenous people often simply left the missions when conditions deteriorated or when "the flow of iron tools dried up" (A.-C. Taylor 1999:222).

There is no mention in existing historical records of the Zápara for the first century of Spanish conquest. However, the seventeenth century was a period of "intensive exploration" in the Ecuadorian Amazon (A.-C. Taylor 1999:223). From 1660 to 1700, the Jesuits undertook "a great wave of expansion in the Curaray-Tigre sector," during which the "bulk of the Zaparoan and Candoan Tribes were contacted" (A.-C. Taylor 1999:223). First recorded contact with the Zápara appears to have been made by Padre Cueva in 1665 (Reeve 1988a:86), below the confluence of the Oas and Curaray rivers (Steward and Métraux 1948:630). In the 1660s other priests noted that the Zápara occupied a swath of jungle from the Curaray to the Corrientes River (Reeve 1988a:86). After the 1660s the Zápara were not mentioned again until 1708, when priests at the mission of San Javier de los Gayes recorded that some Zápara were living there with Gaes and Semigaes, who may have spoken languages related to Zápara (Reeve 1988a:86).

During this period, Zápara from the Bobonaza River area were also absorbed into missions and intermarried with other Indigenous peoples to form the Canelos Kichwa (Obrerem 1974:347; Whitten 1976:7–8). This "colonial tribe" emerged from the "ethnocidal simplification" advocated by the missions: converts from distinct ethnic groups intermarried and were required to use Kichwa (Muratorio 1991:42; see also Hudelson 1985). Priests insisted on Kichwa as the language spoken in their missions, at the same time denying Indigenous inhabitants access to Spanish. This facilitated their control over and conversion of Indigenous inhabitants (Muratorio 1991:38). In 1737 some Zápara were said to have inhabited the Jesuit missions on the Corrientes and Curaray rivers, but many are thought to have avoided the missions (Reeve 1988a:86; Rival 2002:35). Regardless of whether they lived inside or outside the missions, during the eighteenth century, Zápara-speaking populations were dramatically affected by the spread of European diseases. Anne-Christine Taylor (1999:238) estimates that, primarily as a result of disease, the population of the Western Amazon declined by 80 percent between 1550 and 1780. She notes that the Zápara "were one of the chief victims of the disaster, disappearing almost completely, with scarcely more than a few hundred survivors left on the plateau between the Pastaza and the Tigre [rivers]" (A.-C. Taylor 1999:239).

Indigenous peoples did experience some relief when the Spanish ceded control to the newly formed Ecuadorian republic in the early nineteenth century. Their populations likely rebounded during this period, and they regained some of their territories (Erazo 2007:182). Ecuador's independence in 1830 created an "administrative void" in the Oriente because "even the weak controls previously exercised by the royal bureaucracy vanished, and soldiers in search of fortune, traders, a few priests, and adventurers of all kinds 'took over' the region" (Muratorio 1991:72). Historian and ethnographer Blanca Muratorio (1991:72–76, 88) shows that the priests and entrepreneurs who found themselves in the Oriente during the nineteenth century went to the area with competing ideas about Indigenous peoples' role in the regional economy. Jesuit missionaries sought to convert Indigenous people into laborers for church haciendas. In contrast to the Jesuits' insistence on settling Indigenous peoples into villages, traders wanted a flexible, mobile Indigenous labor force for collecting forest goods, as did government administrators who used Indigenous tribute and *repartos* (mandatory labor programs) to enrich themselves: "Jameson (1858:346) estimates that around the 1850s, on completing his term in office a governor could have amassed a sum equivalent to some 6,000 to 8,000 pounds sterling, which was a considerable fortune in Ecuador at that time" (Muratorio 1991:73). Despite the oppressive nature of many forms of elite-mandated Indigenous labor, Muratorio (1991:75–81) argues, competing demands among white elites for Indigenous labor created space for Indigenous people to assert their autonomy—something at which the Zápara were adept.

Zápara-speaking populations increasingly came into contact with outsiders during the nineteenth century, as evidenced by their reference in elites' travel accounts. Italian explorer Gaetano Osculati made numerous mentions of the Zápara in an 1848 account of his travels through eastern Ecuador. He estimated that the "savage nation of the Záparos" consisted of 20,000–25,000 people who inhabited a swath of territory from the Napo River south to the Pastaza (Osculati 2000[1848]:223). James Orton, a professor of natural history at Vassar College, also wrote a brief account of Zápara cultural practice:

> Polygamy is common. They bury in the sitting posture, with the

hammock of the deceased wrapped around him. The very old men are buried with the mouth downward. They make use of the narcotic drink called Ayahuasca, which produces effects similar to those of opium.... There is little social life among them; they never cluster into large villages, but inhabit isolated ranchos. Nomadic in their habits, they wander along the banks of the Napo, between the Andes and the Marañon. They manufacture, from the twisted fibre of the chambiri-palm, most of the twine and hammocks seen in Eastern Ecuador. Their government is patriarchal. (Orton 1876:171–172)

Orton (1876:172) noted that the Zápara were "pacific and hospitable." But in keeping with the social evolutionism of the time, he portrayed them as less advanced than Euro-Americans, noting that they did not have words for numbers above three.

A number of travelers, Osculati and Orton among them (see also Simson 1886), recorded Zápara words and made notes on Zápara grammar. As Orton's assertion suggests, Euro-American explorers and missionaries generally used this information as dubious "proof" of the group's "savagery." The Dominican priest François Pierre (1988[1889]:143), writing about his travels through eastern Ecuador, argued that the simplicity of "savage" Indigenous languages like Zápara signified their speakers' inability to comprehend new ideas or change their ways without external intervention. For Pierre, this underscored the need for these "races of children" to be subject to the tutelage of the Dominican missions that emerged along the Bobonaza and Pastaza rivers in the late nineteenth century.

During the nineteenth century, some Zápara were incorporated into Jesuit and Dominican missions and became "Quichua-speaking, salt-eating, semi-Christians" (Simson 1886:59). Yet, most appear to have lived outside the missions and continued to speak Zápara (Simson 1886:87). Pierre (1988[1889]:186) referred to the Zápara as capricious nomads who, being "fickle by nature," disappeared "quickly and years pass[ed] without hearing anything spoken of them." Throughout much of the colonial and early republican eras, the Zápara were divided between dominant categories of *auca* (wild) and *manso* (tame) Indigenous peoples (Muratorio 1991:108; Reeve 1988a:86; A.-C. Taylor 1999:238). This division was likely advantageous for a portion of the Zápara population because it would have allowed bilingual people to enter or leave the missions at will. It gave "tame" Zápara a position in regional trade networks as go-betweens for "wild" Zápara and other groups: the former provided the latter with manufactured goods in return for the forest goods desired by traders in the region (Erazo 2007:180; A.-C. Taylor 1999:235).

The Rubber Boom

From 1880 to 1914, the Ecuadorian Amazon experienced a boom in natural rubber production that greatly affected the Zápara and other Indigenous peoples (see Stanfield 1998:21). During the late nineteenth century, the source of the world's rubber was the Upper Amazon, and production expanded at a tremendous rate (Whitten 1976:211). Between 1840 and 1900, rubber exports from the Amazon increased from 156 to 25,000 metric tons to meet North American and European demand (Stanfield 1998:21). The expansion of Amazonian rubber production "distorted or supplanted subsistence economies, while new technologies and products opened regions and native peoples to other worlds, often to their detriment" (Stanfield 1998:22). Indigenous people were "cajoled, tricked, and eventually enslaved into service" by *caucheros* (rubber traders) to gather rubber for export to northern industrial countries (Whitten 1976:211; see also Taussig 1987). The rubber boom had such a profound effect on the Napo Kichwa, for example, that they designate it as an epoch (*cauchu uras* [rubber times]) distinct from the rest of history (*callari uras* [beginning times]) (Reeve 1988b:19). In order to protect Amazonian peoples from the abuses of rubber traders, Ecuador's liberal government passed the Special Law of the Oriente in 1899, which recognized Indigenous peoples' rights to government protection.[3] However, government presence in the Oriente was negligible, and no "amount of well-meaning liberal bureaucrats...could...enforce the new legislation with a moderate degree of efficiency" (Muratorio 1991:100). The grievous acts that rubber merchants committed against Indigenous peoples went largely unpunished.

Kichwa from the Napo, Curaray, and Canelos rivers, as well as Kichwa-speaking Zápara—"tame" groups who had a history of working for traders or missionaries—constituted the bulk of the labor force during the rubber boom (Muratorio 1991:109). Caucheros viewed these groups as "usable" labor, in contrast to "wild" groups, who refused to work for the traders (Muratorio 1991:107). Once-distinct groups such as the Gae, Semigae, and Caninche disappeared during the rubber boom (Reeve 1988b:22). Zápara speakers were also hard hit because they occupied territory in eastern Ecuador and Peru where "havoc reigned" at the turn of the century (Whitten 1976:212; see also A.-C. Taylor 1999:239). Traders raided Zápara villages to collect slaves, who were traded downriver, where many were exposed to harsh labor conditions and new diseases.

These hardships are reflected in a story that Domingo, one of the Zápara elders, told me about his family's experiences with rubber traders. Domingo was born after the rubber boom, but his parents worked for a rubber *patrón* (boss). Domingo remembered his father talking about working for months in return for some shabby pieces of clothing or some salt. The people worked "from six in the morning until six at night, because the cauchero hit them very hard. He forced them to work." In addition to physically abusing them, the cauchero forced Juan's family to go "far downriver" into Peru, where they were exposed to unfamiliar diseases that killed the Zápara "little by little." Juan's story highlights the maladies that Zápara suffered during the rubber boom: slave labor, compulsory relocation to areas outside their territory, and unknown diseases.

By the 1910s most Zápara had been killed by slaving raids and epidemics. Records from the Dominican missions in central Pastaza note that in 1909 an outbreak of yellow fever killed many Zápara and that by the 1930s only a few Zápara families were living along the Lliquino and the lower Conambo rivers (León 1937, 1938; Vargas 1937). During the 1920s and 1930s, explorers and anthropologists found little evidence of the Zápara, who numbered no more than a few hundred individuals (Loch 1938:52; Tessman 1999[1930]). The few remaining Zápara married into other ethnic groups and began speaking Kichwa as their primary language (Steward and Métraux 1948:631). When missionaries from the Summer Institute of Linguistics entered Zápara communities along the Conambo River in the early 1950s, they noted that Kichwa was the dominant language and Zápara was spoken by only a few community elders as a private language (Peeke 1962:125).

Shell Oil

During the first half of the twentieth century, Ecuador lost portions of its Amazonian territory to its neighbors. Brazil claimed a part of the Ecuadorian Amazon in 1904, as did Colombia in 1916. In July 1941 Peruvian soldiers invaded Ecuador and established outposts deep within its territory (Whitten 1976:234). In January 1942 the Protocol of Rio de Janeiro ended the border row and granted half of Ecuador's Amazonian territory to Peru.

As the 1941–1942 border war demonstrates, the Ecuadorian state remained absent in the Oriente well into the twentieth century. Most Ecuadorian officials viewed the region as distant and wild and thwarted any substantial plans to colonize it (Stanfield 1998:185). The Ecuadorian state continued to rely on missionaries to "civilize" Indigenous peoples, but also it increasingly turned to oil companies for building a modern infrastructure in the Oriente and making the region economically profitable. In 1937 President Páez (1936–1937) signed a contract with the Anglo-Saxon Pet-roleum Company, "a fictitious front for Royal Dutch Shell" (Martz 1987:48). As historian John Martz (1987:48) notes, Royal Dutch Shell secured "a highly favorable" contract that gave the company access to 10 million hectares of Ecuadorian territory, "exemption from all taxes," and a "royalty rate of merely 5 percent."

Shell was active in the Oriente until 1950, when it left the area for more "readily accessible" oil in the Middle East (Sawyer 2004:232). It encountered difficult conditions for oil exploration in the Oriente and "was in great need of native labor familiar with the forest and used to the hard work of clearing and carrying loads along dangerous and muddy paths" (Muratorio 1991:167). Shell granted short-term, wage-labor contracts to Indigenous men for work as porters. Some Zápara men left their communities to work for Shell, such as Rafael, a Zápara-speaking elder. Although he found the work physically demanding, he thought it better than working for traders or rubber bosses (World War II caused a small boom in Amazonian rubber). Rafael said, "There was no helicopter, so we carried things in and I got to know a lot of different places." Carlos, the Zápara elder mentioned at the beginning of the chapter, left his community as a young man and worked several contracts for Shell, breaking trail and carrying cargo to the oil camps. He was paid 5 sucres (about 70 cents in 1940s dollars) a day, an amount that he now says was not much but that he considered a substantial wage at the time. He also remembers being given good food by the company and a place to stay. Working for Shell also gave Carlos access to an important tool for navigating local economies—Spanish. He learned Spanish in the years he worked for Shell, slowly picking it up from the ingenieros (engineers) employed by the company. They did not know Kichwa, so, according to Carlos, the Indigenous workers had to learn Spanish to communicate with them.

Although Zápara like Carlos became familiar with Spanish during this period, the language never came close to overtaking Kichwa as the primary idiom for community and home life. Rather, the Zápara who learned Spanish were men who left their communities to work—a common practice that continues to this day. After Shell left Ecuador, some men worked on the sugar and tea plantations that sprouted up around Puyo in the 1950s (Whitten 1976:16). Beginning in the 1970s, they also left to work on banana plantations and construction projects in western Ecuador (Muratorio 1991:181; see, for example, Hudelson 1981:222). Family members who had labor experience often helped others to find work and learn some Spanish. One Zápara man, Mauricio, told me that he left his community in the early 1990s to work and earn enough money so that he could start a family. He told me about finding work and learning Spanish, saying that he had a cousin who spoke Spanish and knew that there was good work on the coast. His cousin told him that he "needed to learn Spanish to get by," so Mauricio started to learn from his cousin before leaving for Santo Domingo, where he worked for about two years on construction sites. If he had not done that, he "would not have had money for clothes, for [his] family, or for salt or machetes."

In the 1940s the governor of what was then Napo-Pastaza province claimed that Shell was the solution to the province's "Indian problem"— Indigenous peoples' indebtedness to bosses and semi-nomadic existence, which kept them outside the regular labor pool (Muratorio 1991:169). He thought that working for Shell would help Indigenous people to raise their standard of living and "quiet them down politically" (Muratorio 1991:169). However, Zápara communities remained on the margins of the primary oil-extraction sites and received only sporadic attention from new waves of evangelical missionaries. This situation allowed the Zápara to work when they wished and return to their communities after a few months. However, as oil production, state intervention, and Indigenous activism expanded in the region, the Zápara became more integrated into regional and national political economies.

Colonization and Indigenous Organization

"Ecuador was, is, and will be an Amazonian country." This quote began to appear on government letterhead in the 1970s and marks a watershed in the history of the Ecuadorian Amazon (Radcliffe 2001:134). Commercial oil production in the Oriente began in 1972 when the international price of petroleum was booming. Coastal and highland elites saw the Oriente's vast and untapped mineral wealth as the key to Ecuador's modernization, and the state initiated efforts to incorporate the region (Radcliffe 2001:134; Radcliffe and Westwood 1996:65). On September 15, 1972, President Rodríguez Lara (1972–1976) gave a speech in Puyo outlining his plan for national development in the Oriente. The first component was the expansion of the area's infrastructure and public services crucial to improving communication and increasing commerce in the Oriente (Whitten 1976:265). The second was "acceleration in small-scale commercial production and improved land utilization" (Whitten 1976:266). This attention to the Oriente stood in dramatic contrast to prior histories of elite neglect and state absence.

The state encouraged Ecuadorians from the highlands and the coast to settle the Amazonian lowlands (figure 2.4), by designating Indigenous territories as *tierras baldías* (barren or uninhabited lands) under the 1964

Figure 2.4 View of the Baños-Puyo Road. This road served as an important route for settlers heading into the Amazon from the Andes. Photo by author.

Law of Agrarian Reform and Colonization. The law abolished "archaic social relations of production characteristic of the countryside," such as servile labor, known as *huasipungo* (Crain 1990:47; see also Velasco Abad 1983; Zamosc 1994). However, the reform led to an almost insignificant redistribution of land to Indigenous peasants (Sawyer 2004:44; Waters 2007:126). Hacienda owners reduced the size of their landholdings, often selling the least productive land and focusing on semi-mechanized dairy production that required fewer workers than did traditional crops (Waters 2007:121). For example, only 3 percent of the land in Chimborazo province was redistributed to peasants between 1964 and 1970 (Korovkin 1997:28–32). More than redistributing land, the agrarian reform encouraged internal colonialism in the Amazon, easing land shortages in the Sierra that were fueled by population growth (Sawyer 1997:68; Uquillas 1984). To this end, the government created the Instituto Ecuatoriano de Reforma Agraria y Colonización (Ecuadorian Institute of Agrarian Reform and Colonization, or IERAC), which aided internal settlers in establishing legal title to Amazonian land. The state viewed colonists as agents of national development—"real" Ecuadorians who would settle the Amazon and make it agriculturally "productive" (Radcliffe and Westwood 1996:124). As one colonist in the northern Oriente claimed, "before the colonizers came, this wasn't Ecuador, this wasn't Colombia, it wasn't anything" (Radcliffe and Westwood 1996:124).

In contrast to *campesino* (peasant), the word used in the highlands, by the 1970s *Indio* (Indian) and *Indígena* (Indigene) were used almost exclusively in referring to Indigenous peoples in the Oriente, as a means to exclude them from emerging notions of Ecuadorian citizenship (Albó 2004:20; Radcliffe and Westwood 1996:69). Ecuador's National Culture Law of 1972 stated that all Ecuadorians were part Indigenous—insinuating that "completely Indigenous" people were not Ecuadorian (Albó 2004:21). This provided a not-so-subtle rationale for refusing to acknowledge Indigenous land tenure in the Amazon. Colonization in the Amazon was extensive: 4.5 million hectares were awarded to settlers between 1964 and 1994 (Sawyer 2004:44). Settlers cleared forest for cattle grazing and crop production and displaced Indigenous people, pushing them farther into the forest (Yashar 2005:113).

Oil extraction also imperiled Indigenous livelihoods and ecosystems. Ecuador's switch to an oil-based economy was quick and had a tumultuous effect on many of the region's Indigenous peoples. Exploration and production moved the frontier of colonization farther into the forest, affecting more and more communities (Kimmerling 1993; Whitten 1976:252–263). Oil companies expanded roads and created airstrips in remote jungle communities, providing colonists and missionaries with easier access to Indigenous territory (figure 2.5) (see, for example, A.-C. Taylor 1981:649). Indigenous responses to colonization and oil extraction were localized at first and involved communities that were directly affected by colonization (Whitten 1976:245–248; Yashar 2005:116–117). However, local community associations collaborated soon thereafter, laying the foundations for provincial and regional organizations (Yashar 2005:99, 129).

Scholars often point to the Shuar, located in the southeastern province of Morona-Santiago, as the first group in Latin America to organize exclusively along ethnic lines (see, for example, Brysk 2000:8; García and Lucero 2004:166; Yashar 2005:119). Despite various attempts by Catholic priests to establish a mission in their territory, the Shuar remained relatively independent from state and church influence well into the twentieth century. In 1887 the Dominicans built a mission in Shuar territory, which they abandoned in 1898. In 1924 Salesian missionaries entered Shuar territory, constructed several missions, and began to settle the Shuar into village *centros* (centers) with schools (Harner 1972:30). Initial colonization was sparse, consisting primarily of families who followed the Salesians and settled around the mission in Sucúa, south of the provincial capital of Macas (Erazo 2007:187). Pressure on Shuar lands increased during the 1950s and 1960s, however, as new waves of settlers entered the area. Worried that the Shuar would leave the mission centros and retreat into the forest (Hendricks 1991:56), Salesian missionaries worked with the communities to organize and petition for titles to their land (Salazar 1977). In 1964 the Salesians helped the Shuar from Sucúa and other centros in Morona-Santiago to form

Figure 2.5 Unloading sacks of rice on the airstrip in Llanchamacocha. Small runways serve as important means for connecting Indigenous organizations in Puyo with their constituents in far-off rain forest communities. Photo by author.

the state-recognized Federación Shuar (Shuar Federation). Additionally, Salesian missionaries gave them cattle and credit to begin commercial ranching.[4] Yet Salesian influence in the organization quickly declined as Shuar leaders became more and more confident, pushing their own agenda of land tenure and bilingual education (Hendricks 1991:57).

Anthropologist Juliet Erazo (2007:181) argues that many scholars contrast the Shuar to highland Kichwa because of the Shuar's oft-cited acts of resistance and early adoption of ethnic-based organization.[5] As such, the history of the Shuar often "comes to represent that of the entire Ecuadorian Oriente" (Erazo 2007:181). Yet Erazo (2007:190–192) notes that lowland Kichwa in Napo and Pastaza provinces played an important role in elaborating Indigenous rights demands in the region. Early efforts at Kichwa organizing were often formed around pragmatic issues of collective land titling, economic development, and autonomy from Catholic missions (Yashar 2005:123). In 1969 several Kichwa communities formed the Federación Provincial de Organizaciones Campesinas de Napo (Provincial Federation of Peasant Organizations of Napo, or FEPOCAN), which later changed its name to the Federación de Organizaciones Indígenas del Napo (Federation of Indigenous Organizations of Napo, or FOIN). Like the Shuar, FOIN used existing government channels to petition for land titles—a strategy that required Shuar and Napo Kichwa communities to demonstrate that they were "*working* the land" through ranching or market-oriented farming (Yashar 2005:126).

In 1978 young Kichwa leaders formed the Organización de Pueblos Indígenas de Pastaza (Organization of Indigenous Peoples of Pastaza, or OPIP). As a "second generation" organization, OPIP drew less on church-based networks than did its predecessors and more on collaboration with Kichwa and Shuar leaders (Yashar 2005:126). However, as political scientist Deborah Yashar (2005:126) notes, OPIP's approach differed from the latter in several important regards. First, it was a provincial organization, meaning that, instead of representing a single ethnic group, it claimed representation of all the Indigenous peoples in Pastaza province. Second, OPIP leaders argued that Indigenous peoples had a right to land, whether this was being put to "productive use or not, that was derived from historical-use territories, not contemporary legal structures" (Sawyer 1997:69–70). This was an important move in challenging the dominance of state-administered understandings of Indigenous citizenship and rights and served as the basis for Indigenous peoples' future land claims.

In 1980 FOIN, OPIP, and the Shuar Federation founded the Confederación de Nacionalidades Indígenas de la Amazonía Ecuatoriana (Confederation of Indigenous Nationalities of the Ecuadorian Amazon, or CONFENIAE) to coordinate their efforts at a regional level. CONFENIAE was the first Indigenous organization in Ecuador to employ the term *nacionalidad* (nationality). Amazonian leaders utilized the concept as a foundation for an "ethnic" alternative to existing organizational units, such as unions and cooperatives (Lucero 2003:32–33, 2007:217). Each nationality has its own language, culture, economy, and history—all of which are intricately linked to a particular territory. Throughout the 1980s and 1990s, CONFENIAE increasingly used this idea to redraw the political map of the

Oriente, pushing the Ecuadorian government to recognize the national territories of particular Indigenous peoples and grant them control over those territories' resources (see Sawyer 2004:46–47). As part of this political project, CONFENIAE leaders worked to organize all the Indigenous peoples in the Ecuadorian Amazon into nationalities, helping smaller groups such as the Waorani and Cofán to found their own organizations (Selverston-Scher 2001:34). This process has not been without its difficulties. Newly organized groups found themselves at a disadvantage in comparison with more seasoned organizations, whose leaders had more experience and better access to bilingual education and therefore "stood in a privileged position vis-à-vis the state and had better access to development monies and government posts" (Erazo 2007:181). Nonetheless, collaboration among nationalities in the confederation was strong in the 1980s and 1990s, and it made significant gains in bilingual education and land titling.

A Zápara Nationality Emerges

In relation to many of the other Indigenous nationalities in the Ecuadorian Amazon, the Zápara were late in organizing. They were part of what one might call a "third generation" of Indigenous organizations that emerged in the late 1980s and 1990s to represent small nationalities. Unlike the Kichwa and Shuar, the Zápara communities did not face immediate pressure from internal settlement and oil extraction because they were located some distance from the colonization frontier.

Zápara elders who lived in the Kichwa community of Sarayaku (which has a long history of militant Indigenous activism and opposition to oil extraction) often talked about their involvement in the early stages of organizing OPIP. Although these elders eventually returned to the Conambo River area, the Zápara maintained links with Sarayaku and OPIP during the 1980s and 1990s. During the early 1990s, several men and women from Llanchamacocha married people from Sarayaku and participated in OPIP's 1992 march (discussed in chapter 3), when OPIP leaders demanded that roughly 70 percent of Pastaza province be divided into Indigenous territories (Sawyer 2004:27). According to OPIP's proposal, each nationality in Pastaza would be awarded its own territory (Sawyer 2004:48).

Following the march, President Borja (1988–1992) gave Indigenous communities titles to more than 1 million hectares of land in Pastaza province. The government responded that it only awarded "land"—not territories—and that it would only "do so with 'ethnic' groups"—not Indigenous nationalities (Sawyer 2004:48). It considered OPIP's framework of nationalities and territories a "subversive" attempt to create an Indigenous state within the Ecuadorian nation and granted only 55 percent of the area demanded by OPIP (Sawyer 2004:49). The Borja government divided this area into nineteen land blocks, each of which was given an "Indigenous" name by Ecuadorian officials to create the "illusion that each...corresponded to locally recognized social divisions" (Sawyer 2004:51). Moreover, the state maintained its right to subterranean resources within Indigenous land blocks and made it illegal for their inhabitants to impede oil extraction. Many Indigenous leaders believed that the government land titles were meant to divide Indigenous peoples in Pastaza province so that it would be easier "for oil companies to negotiate directly with Indigenous communities" rather than with experienced Indigenous leaders from OPIP (Yashar 2005:128).

Land block no. 6 was deemed the Comuna Záparo (Záparo Commune), although it included only a small portion of the land that OPIP attributed to the Zápara nationality (see Sawyer 2004:47). The boundaries of the Comuna Záparo block run approximately from the middle of the Conambo and Pindoyacu rivers to a point 40 km away from the Peruvian border, stopping at what used to be the beginning of the security zone along Ecuador's border with Peru. French anthropologist Anne-Gaël Bilhaut (2005:8) observes that only 5 percent of the individuals within block no. 6 self-identify as Zápara. In short, the territory was an administrative fiction; 95 percent of its five hundred inhabitants identify as Kichwa and Achuar. In contrast, Bilhaut (2005:9) estimates that 90 percent of those individuals who self-identify as Zápara live outside the official boundaries of the Comuna Záparo.

In 1996 people from the Comuna Záparo formed the Union de Centros de Territorio Záparo del Ecuador (Union of the Centers of the Záparo Territory of Ecuador, or UCTZE) with aid from the Asociación de Indígenas Evangélicos de Pastaza Región Amazónica (Association of Evangelical Indians of Pastaza in the Amazonian Region, or AIEPRA). In 1997 UCTZE became the Organización de la Nacionalidad Záparo del Ecuador (Organization of the Záparo Nationality of Ecuador, or ONAZE), which I refer to as the Comuna Záparo for the remainder of the book. Through interviews with community members and an analysis of organizational documents, Bilhaut (2005:9–10) concludes that the people who formed UCTZE appropriated the name *Záparo* as a reference to their location within the Comuna Záparo; they were not interested in forming a Zápara nationality because they did not identify as such. Bilhaut (2005:9) asserts that many people in the Comuna Záparo opposed the formation of ONAZE, which they claimed was motivated by a few leaders who wanted to form a Zápara nationality for their own personal gain. The situation is perhaps not as clear-cut as Bilhaut's statistics would suggest, though, and care must be taken here to indicate that many people along the lower Conambo have legitimate claims to Zápara identity. A number of the historical sources cited in this chapter indicate the presence of Zápara populations in this area during the nineteenth and early twentieth centuries.

ONAZE is significant because it was the first organization to claim Zápara identity in Ecuador. Moreover, the people along the Upper Conambo with whom I worked claim to have organized in response to ONAZE, which they said was wrongfully appropriating Zápara identity. In 1997 people from the communities of Llanchamacocha, Jandiayacu, Mazaramu, and Cuyacocha came together to build an organization that would protect and recuperate Zápara identity and culture. Leaders who were present at that meeting said that the discussion revolved around the revalorization of Zápara heritage, which they believed made them the rightful claimants of Zápara identity in comparison with the Comuna Zápara. Those assembled also discussed the rebirth of a Zápara nationality with its own territory and control over its own schools, education, and development. The following year, the four communities formed the Asociación de la Nacionalidad Zápara de la Provincia de Pastaza (Association of the Zápara Nationality of Pastaza Province, or ANAZPPA).

ANAZPPA was initially organized with encouragement and assistance from OPIP, which provided office space for the Zápara in Puyo. At the time of their organization's foundation, Zápara leaders had little political experience and almost no economic or organizational resources; aid from OPIP was crucial in ensuring that the organization got off the ground. In 2002 ANAZPPA officially separated from OPIP, forming the Organización de la Nacionalidad Zápara del Ecuador (Organization of the Zápara Nationality of Ecuador, or ONZAE), which became NAZAE (Nacionalidad Zápara del Ecuador) in 2003. Although the Zápara have maintained close ties to OPIP, NAZAE leaders felt that their communities' political aspirations and needs were marginalized within OPIP, which had transformed from a provincial umbrella organization to one that primarily represented the Kichwa nationality. NAZAE leaders saw the formation of a Zápara nationality as an important means for strengthening their voice within regional politics and negotiating more directly with the state. This move was supported by CONFENIAE and OPIP because the creation of new Indigenous nationalities supported the notion that Ecuador is plurinational while broadening the number of peoples who could claim separate territories from the state. A number of Indigenous organizations and government ministries have acknowledged NAZAE (and its prior incarnations) as the primary representative of the Zápara nationality in Ecuador (see Bilhaut 2005:10; Viatori

2007:111). However, as I explain in the next chapter, people from the Comuna Záparo have repeatedly contested this recognition of NAZAE as the legitimate representative of the Zápara nationality in Ecuador.

Conclusion

Since first contact with Spanish missionaries and administrators, Zápara people have adapted their practice, language use, and identity to the impositions of external political economies and elite conceptualizations of Indigeneity. Most recently, communities along the Conambo and Pindoyacu rivers adapted their identity to fit emerging discourses of Indigenous organization by emphasizing their distinctness from neighboring Indigenous communities. By doing so, the Zápara have been able to enter not only into regional and national Indigenous organizational discourses but also into state discourses of Indigeneity, which stress cultural rights based on the expression of local differences.

Throughout the remainder of this book, I explore the Záparas' process of self-organization and the changes this shift has engendered in local Zápara identities and political activism. The following chapters demonstrate the importance of the idea of nationalities for creating new political openings for the Zápara. However, they also show how this process has involved a complex refashioning of Zápara identity to fit a model of political participation that has been shaped and appropriated by a plurality of political actors, from regional Indigenous organizations to the World Bank (Almeida 2005).

Anthropologist Theodore Macdonald (2002:183) suggests that "plurinationalism existed in the traditionally ethnic (and linguistic) distinctions in the Amazon region." With its emphasis on regional and local cultural differences, the concept of nationality perhaps fits better in the linguistically diverse Amazon than in the (seemingly) less diverse Andes (see Lucero 2003:38). However, the idea of nationality never reflected what "was really there" in regards to Indigenous organization and ethnicity in any region of Ecuador (Lucero 2007:217). Rather, Indigenous leaders' use of the term emerged from their desire to articulate new ways of conceptualizing inclusion and political participation in Ecuador (Lucero 2003, 2007). Although this reframing has been an effective means for addressing Indigenous demands to the state, it has also proved to be a difficult transformation for some organizations as they have sought to take "what is there" and make it into "what should be there." This has been especially true for the Zápara, whose emergence as an independent nationality has been tricky, given their history of multilingualism, displacement, and cultural assimilation. The following chapters explore how the creation of a Zápara nationality has involved the selective inclusion and exclusion of different aspects of local identities, histories, and practices, simultaneously producing novel opportunities and limitations for Zápara activism.

3 Zápara Leaders and Self-Representation

The NAZAE office bustled with an unusual amount of energy on April 15, 2003. The day before, several leaders from the Kichwa community of Sarayaku had been arrested for protests against oil company incursions in their territory. OPIP claimed that the arrests were unfounded and unconstitutional and called on other Indigenous organizations for support. In response, the Zápara readied for a public protest in downtown Puyo. People scurried about the NAZAE office, donning vests made from tree fiber, necklaces of animal teeth and seeds, and feathered headdresses. Before leaving the office, several men also grabbed spears.

The sight of half a dozen Zápara carrying spears down Puyo's main street drew long stares and pointing from several onlookers. After crossing a couple of blocks, the Zápara were greeted at the entrance to the prosecutor's office by a large crowd of protestors, most of whom were from Sarayaku, although leaders from other nationalities were present as well. Eventually, the protestors gained entry. Once inside the small and stuffy office, Indigenous leaders addressed their grievances to the prosecutor. As a local camera crew recorded the exchanges, leaders stepped forward and denounced the arrests of their fellow activists. The Záparas' president, Bartolo Ushigua, was one of the last to speak. Standing before the prosecutor, he was adorned with a feathered headdress and wore a large beaded necklace. His attire provided a striking visual contrast to the business suit of the government official as he introduced himself in Zápara and Kichwa before denouncing the arrests in Spanish. The visual sign of his headdress and clothing marked Bartolo as culturally different from the mestizo official he addressed, and his use of Zápara and Kichwa symbolically framed his message as Indigenous.

Since its official organization in 1998, the Zápara nationality has relied on a small group of multilingual activists like Bartolo to advance its agenda and revalorize Zápara identity. In short, the activists have been charged with the task of securing recognition for the Zápara nationality—the all-important "first step towards demanding rights and protecting resources" (Hodgson 2002:1041; see also C. Taylor 1994). This has been difficult, given the Záparas' history of social upheaval and cultural assimilation, which have produced the nationality's current linguistic and cultural hybridity. In Amazonian Ecuador, the primary marker of a nationality is its language. Although a portion of each nationality is bilingual—something that is encouraged by Indigenous-administered education programs in Indigenous languages and Spanish (see chapter 4)—each nationality is delineated from the others by the use of a unique language: Kichwa is the language of the Kichwa nationality, Wao Teredo is the language of the Waorani nationality, and so on. CONFENIAE and its member organizations have asserted that language is the most tangible evidence of the continuity of Indigenous societies in the Amazon from the pre-contact era to the present. This continuity provides a foundation for Indigenous peoples' claims to special rights as Indigenous Ecuadorians.

Given this, the difficulty the Zápara faced was that—after generations of assimilation and intermarriage with other nationalities, mostly with Kichwa—they spoke languages (Kichwa and Spanish) that were not specific or unique to their nationality's identity and history. The problem in their return was that they were too affected by colonialism and were "caught up between a 'thick' past and a 'thin' present" (Lazzari 2003:60). They did not fit the emergent parameters of Indigenous identity in the Ecuadorian Amazon, given the absence of their own national language. In order to mitigate this and present a public image of the Zápara nationality that conformed to official notions of Indigenous culture, Bartolo and his NAZAE colleagues focused on the endangered Zápara language as the most tangible representation of their nationality's cultural difference.

In the role of spokespeople, Zápara activists served as symbols of the nationality they represented. Public encounters like the one in the prosecutor's office constituted important moments for Zápara activists to reinforce the uniqueness of their communities' identities by utilizing aspects of their material culture and linguistic repertoire that most visibly summarized their difference from national Ecuadorian society. An influential body of literature on Latin American Indigenous movements has demonstrated how Indigenous leaders have strategically played to dominant notions of "exotic" Indigenous culture to advance their political demands. Anthropologists, for example, have focused on Indigenous spokespeople's public performances of cultural difference in ways that accord with Northern misconceptions of "real Indians" as a means for securing support from influential donors (see, for example, Conklin and Graham 1995; Jackson 1995; Turner 1991).

In this chapter, I examine the ways in which Indigenous activists represented Zápara identity in their attempts to garner support from an array of non-Zápara outsiders. However, I argue that these activists did not function simply as cultural translators who reformulated Zápara identity in a manner that fit broad stereotypes of Indigenous identity, to serve as "bridges" between Indigenous and non-Indigenous cultures (Karttunnen 1994:300). Rather, I argue that Zápara activists engaged in the process of redefining cultural difference and articulating new spaces for the expression of Indigenous identity (Lauer 2006). In the process of reshaping Zápara identity to fit emergent paradigms of Indigenous identity, NAZAE activists creatively re-adapted aspects of local linguistic practice to communicate Zápara political demands to outside audiences (see Graham 2002:214). In so doing, they expanded the acceptable boundaries of language use and Indigenous identity in public encounters between Indigenous leaders and non-Indigenous interlocutors. However, in the process of presenting Zápara national identity to non-Zápara, NAZAE activists also excluded aspects of Zápara identity and practice that did not fit within current discourses of multiculturalism and plurinationalism (see Mallon 1995:285; Warren 1998:26). This was particularly evident in NAZAE activists' criticism of rival Zápara leaders' purported cultural "corruption" and linguistic hybridity.

Zápara Dirigentes

Before discussing Zápara self-representation, it is necessary first to sketch who the Zápara leaders were. In a simple sense, they were the individuals who ran NAZAE—coordinating bilingual education, negotiating with government agencies, and working with NGOs to implement development projects. At any one time, this group numbered around a dozen individuals, each of whom had a specific position in the organization (either in the overall administration as a president or vice president, as the head of one of the organization's programs, or as the director of a specific project), for which he or she received a small stipend. These individuals were considered leaders within the Zápara communities because of their abilities to articulate Zápara political demands to non-Zápara audiences. Although sometimes trained in traditional leadership roles (as healers, for example), dirigentes were different from community leaders (kurakas in Kichwa and akamenos in Zápara) in that their authority was rooted not in local kinship ties, but in knowledge of external politics and state bureaucracies (Lauer 2006:53).

In a number of ways, Zápara dirigentes were similar to what the Italian political philosopher Antonio Gramsci (1971a:13) referred to as organic intellectuals.[1] Gramsci thought of intellectuals as any individuals who "have...a responsibility to produce knowledge and/or instill that knowledge into others...so that a given way of seeing the world is reproduced" (Crehan 2002:131–132; Gramsci 1971b:8). Organic intellectuals work to direct "the ideas and aspirations of the class to which they organically belong" (Gramsci 1971b:3). They are fundamental to the process of organizing emerging social classes because they are responsible for transforming "the incoherent and fragmentary 'feelings' of those who live a particular class position into a coherent and reasoned account of the world as it appears from that position" (Crehan 2002:130). Put another way, organic intellectuals are engaged in the process of articulating and organizing the worldview of subordinate groups in a manner that constructs an alternative to existing forms of hegemony.

The NAZAE leaders whom I studied all came from rural Amazonian communities, and many were involved in founding the organization. These leaders were the primary agents in the representation of Zápara culture and identity. As such, they were responsible for articulating a political narrative that united their communities behind a reinvigorated Zápara identity and disseminating this narrative through multilingual education programs and pan-community reunions. Additionally, they occupied an important "channeling" role (Gramsci 1971b:10), representing their communities' political demands in a manner that resonated with regional and national multicultural discourses, as well as negotiating with state and non-state actors for recognition and resources.

Zápara constituents referred to NAZAE activists as *dirigentes* (leaders), whether they were speaking in Spanish or Kichwa. The concept of dirigentes—semi-professional individuals charged with representing local political demands to powerful actors and institutions—is relatively new in the Zápara communities, and an equivalent in Zápara or Kichwa has yet to emerge. All the dirigentes knew Spanish and had some formal education. Most had attended only primary school, but a few had *colegio* (high school) or *escuela normal* (normal school—a training course for teachers) degrees. Completion of such a degree represented an important milestone for NAZAE and its dirigentes. As such, it was often marked by a celebration that extended late into the night and involved chicha, *maito* (meat and yucca wrapped in a banana leaf and broiled in an open fire), and an elaborate cake from one of Puyo's downtown bakers.

Not all the dirigentes who worked in NAZAE identified themselves as Zápara. During my research, I met three individuals who self-identified as Kichwa. One was married to a Zápara woman. The other two were teachers who were able to find steady work with NAZAE at a time when the small organization was short on educated activists. All three had been engaged in other community-level activism in Pastaza and shared the political goals of their Zápara colleagues. However, these dirigentes were not involved in publicly representing NAZAE (see Rappaport 2005:57–58). Rather, they worked on the curriculum for the Zápara schools: training teachers, documenting the Zápara language, and writing multilingual workbooks.

All of NAZAE's dirigentes did, however, speak Kichwa as their first language. Some who had lived in Puyo for years and worked as teachers were quite proficient in Spanish. Others were less comfortable with it—they made grammatical errors, spoke with heavy Kichwa accents, and possessed only basic literacy. Working in NAZAE has been an important way of improving Spanish fluency and literacy for many Zápara who did not have access to good primary or secondary education. They learned on the job as they assisted more experienced dirigentes. There was a core of six to eight professional dirigentes who lived in Puyo and worked full-time for NAZAE. The rest were men from the Zápara communities who occupied different positions on a rotating basis for six months to two years. Working in NAZAE gave men a preferable alternative to occasional cash labor in the Sierra or Costa. Moreover, it familiarized them with the basics of Indigenous organizing. The presence of community members in NAZAE also kept the more professional dirigentes abreast of local concerns. It was one means to strengthen the often tenuous connection between NAZAE and the far-off Zápara communities. However, Zápara working in NAZAE on a temporary basis were clearly subordinate to the more permanent leaders, who were fluent in Spanish and more politically savvy. This caused community members working in NAZAE to grumble that Bartolo and the other seasoned activists excluded others from taking an active role in governing the organization. Conversely, permanent NAZAE activists sometimes complained that their more temporary counterparts possessed such limited skills and political ambitions that they were more of a burden than a help.

I mention above that Zápara men left the communities to work in NAZAE. This is no mistake. The role of dirigente was a predominantly male domain. Throughout my research with NAZAE, women rarely occupied any of the central decision-making positions within the organization, such as president or vice president. Women were often excluded from important meetings with other Indigenous dirigentes over issues of territorial boundaries and collective political actions. In May 2003 I attended a meeting between Zápara and Pastaza Kichwa leaders in Quito to discuss the border between the nationalities' territories. Although the group of NAZAE staff that arrived for the meeting consisted of men and women, the women waited outside the office while the men discussed the issue at hand.

The gendered nature of NAZAE politics has been the result of an ongoing interaction between local and national understandings of gender (see Muratorio 1998). Within Zápara social discourse, gender complimentarity is stressed as an *ideal* in the sense that "life is not possible without masculine–feminine combinations" (Uzendoski 2005:45). In reality, however, there is an asymmetry in gender relations that privileges men. Moreover, in the process of becoming politically active, the Zápara adopted existing forms of Indigenous organization and rights discourses that often gloss over enduring gender disparities. The "collective rights demanded by the [Ecuadorian Indigenous] confederations are presented as gender-neutral," despite significant socioeconomic differences between Indigenous men and women (Radcliffe 2002:161). Women are often featured as icons of Indigenous cultural difference because they are constructed as being more "traditional" than their male counterparts (Radcliffe 2002:161; Weismantel 2001).[2] However, women have occupied crucial "supporting roles" in Indigenous organizing—answering phones, coordinating the logistics of community reunions and training workshops, and tracking the receipts and paperwork for projects (Hernández Castillo 2006:233). Moreover, despite the limitations that gendered notions of Indigenous identity place on women activists, some women have reworked these notions to their advantage by using their status as icons of Indigenous tradition to position themselves as "close to incorruptible" interpreters of public politics (Farthing 2007:8–9; Hernández Castillo 2006:239).

An example of the latter is María, a dirigente who had been active in NAZAE since its founding in 1998. Throughout my research, María did not occupy any of the central positions in the organization's administration. She was the director of women's issues for a period and then headed the (somewhat nonoperational) Zápara tourism program. Nonetheless, María created a position of influence in NAZAE by situating herself as a more "truthful" judge of organizational politics than her male counterparts (Farthing 2007). Because of the large geographical distance between the Zápara communities and the NAZAE office in Puyo, disagreements and misunderstandings between the communities and NAZAE leaders erupted on a regular basis. María took advantage of this gap by inserting herself as NAZAE's emissary in the communities, smoothing out problems and building consensus among community leaders for NAZAE projects. She also gained influence with NGOs and journalists who had worked with the Zápara by stressing her "traditionalism," care for culture and the environment, and disdain for monetary gain. She traveled to New York and San Francisco to speak at

Indigenous and women's forums and was featured in international media coverage of Zápara cultural revitalization and rain forest preservation. Albeit excluded from a central role in NAZAE, María created space for herself as an influential political actor because her status as an Indigenous woman conferred heightened authenticity. It was an option that was not available to most Zápara women, who—unlike María, whose parents had sent her to a missionary school—were not proficient in Spanish.

Despite the internal heterogeneity, NAZAE dirigentes presented a "unified political voice" to non-Zápara outsiders (Rappaport 2005:58). Yet, crafting a homogenous public image of Zápara culture was no easy task, given the many differences within NAZAE and the Zápara nationality. I now turn to an examination of the challenges this presented for NAZAE leaders.

Strategies of Self-Representation

In a study of Brazilian Indigenous leaders, anthropologist Laura Graham (2002:182–183,190) argues that non-Indigenous audiences assume a direct link between the language that an Indigenous representative speaks and his or her membership in a particular cultural group. Indigenous language is one of the most tangible emblems of Indians' cultural difference from non-Indigenous society and is "positively valued" by many non-Indigenous audiences as symbolizing a lack of cultural "contamination" or foreign influence (Graham 2002:188–189). As such, Graham (2002:197) suggests that Indigenous languages function as important tools for Indigenous leaders to index their authenticity when interacting with non-Indigenous publics. Yet, Graham (2002:189–205) argues that, given the multifunctionality of language, it is not possible simply to say that an Indigenous leader's use of an Indigenous language symbolizes authenticity to outside audiences. Nor does a leader's use of a language such as Portuguese or Spanish mark him or her as illegitimate to non-Indigenous audiences. In addition to symbolizing a speaker's identity, language conveys a message through particular sounds and grammatical forms. Graham asserts that Indigenous languages are important symbols of speakers' legitimacy before non-Indigenous audiences but are limited in their capability to communicate important messages to these audiences. Graham (2002:205) identifies three strategies that Indigenous spokespeople use in Brazil to balance the symbolic and communicative functions of different languages: bracketing speech in non-Indigenous languages with Indigenous phrases and linguistic performances, using translators, and invoking identifiably Indigenous imagery when speaking in Portuguese.

The Zápara language has been an effective symbol for the Zápara to assert their ethnic difference within regional and national politics. When speaking publicly, Zápara dirigentes used the Zápara language to validate their political goals, their identity, and the credibility of what they said as Indigenous. But given the necessity of bilingualism in public encounters, Zápara dirigentes employed linguistic strategies similar to those outlined by Graham. Within the context of contemporary Ecuadorian Indigenous politics, leaders who speak Spanish "too" fluently are sometimes viewed with suspicion by Indigenous and non-Indigenous audiences alike. Anthropologist Janet Hendricks (1991:63) in her work on the Shuar notes that, as a result of this skepticism, Shuar leaders sometimes denied their knowledge of Spanish. When addressing outside audiences, Zápara dirigentes used Zápara phrases as a way to bracket their narratives in Spanish, ensuring that the content of these narratives was perceived as Indigenous. However, the Zápara language alone was not an effective marker of these dirigentes' legitimacy because their knowledge of the language was limited. In order to get around this issue, Zápara dirigentes employed a variety of performative linguistic and paralinguistic strategies. They combined Zápara words and phrases with Kichwa. When speaking in Spanish, they tapped into internationally circulating tropes such as Indigenous environmental stewardship and opposition to "Western" encroachment.

Bartolo, NAZAE's president, used these strategies in his role as the main spokesperson for the Zápara nationality. During his presidency, from 1998 to 2005, he spoke at public events and gave interviews to newspaper and television journalists in Ecuador and abroad. As the following examples demonstrate, Bartolo creatively combined Zápara, Kichwa, and "traditional" clothes to symbolize his authenticity as an Indigenous Zápara leader.

Bartolo was fluent in Spanish and Kichwa but had a limited knowledge of Zápara. He began most of his public addresses with the phrase *Kwijia ikicha sápara ñanuka*. He would first tell his audience that this sentence was in Zápara before translating it into Spanish as *Yo soy un hombre de la selva* (I am a man of the rain forest), which allowed him to capitalize on the symbolism of an Indigenous grammar and phonology (Graham 2002:207). This was the case in an address Bartolo gave in Barcelona, as reported in the Spanish newspaper *El País* (2001). Bartolo began with the "I am a man of the rain forest" introduction. He then switched to speaking in Spanish about Indigenous rights such as bilingual education and health. He intertwined his discussion of the Záparas' political concerns with fragments of Zápara stories and a juxtaposition of his life in the Ecuadorian rain forest with life in urban Barcelona. According to the *El País* article, he commented on how odd it was to be in a place like the city of Barcelona, where he had to "pay for something to eat." By doing so, Bartolo ensured that the content of his

Figure 3.1 NAZAE dirigentes, one dressed in a llanchama bark vest and feather headdress, on their way to a CONFENIAE meeting. Photo by author.

narrative was received as "Indigenous," even if the linguistic channel was not. To the same end, he also wore a vest made out of bark from the *llanchama* (poulsenia armata) tree, which Zápara historically have used to fashion clothes (figure 3.1).

In addition to utilizing aspects of Zápara material culture and language, dirigentes incorporated community members into their public performances as symbols of Zápara cultural "purity." The surviving Zápara-speaking elders were particularly important emblems of Zápara cultural legitimacy, and their ability to speak Zápara served as a powerful symbol of the nationality's linguistic difference. On May 19, 2003, there was a celebration in the NAZAE office of the two-year anniversary of UNESCO's recognition of the Zápara language. A representative from UNESCO's Quito office came with several Ecuadorian journalists, who recorded the event for local television news. Roughly twenty Zápara were present, many of whom wore llanchama bark clothing over their button-down shirts and jeans. The small celebration began with the UNESCO representative congratulating the Zápara on their work to preserve their language and promising his continuing support. Bartolo responded by thanking the UNESCO representative in Spanish and speaking about the progress the Zápara were making in reintroducing the language into their communities. He then switched to Kichwa to ask two Zápara elders present to speak on behalf of their communities. One of the elders, an older woman from one of the Conambo River communities, sang in Zápara. She was followed by the other elder, a man from the Pindoyacu River region, who gave a short greeting in Zápara. Both elders self-translated into Kichwa, and Bartolo then translated their words into Spanish for the UNESCO representative and the journalists.

Zápara dirigentes often asked elders to speak at public events like this. Alternatively, the dirigentes sometimes showed non-Zápara audiences video recordings of the elders speaking Zápara. In these videos, the elders were presented as the "true voice of the rain forest" (Graham 2002:193), which could only be expressed through Zápara. To ensure that these voices remained "uncorrupted," Zápara dirigentes served as translators to Spanish for elders, even for those who spoke some Spanish, thus emphasizing the "otherness" of the Zápara speakers. In October 2000 Bartolo visited universities and nonprofit organizations in California, showing a short film about the revitalization of the Zápara language. The film focused on the Zápara elders from the communities of Llanchamacocha, Jandiayacu, and Mazaramu who spoke or sang in Zápara. Bartolo functioned as the main translator in the film. In Spanish, he conveyed the elders' concerns about the transmission of their language and Zápara mythology to future generations (the film was subtitled in English for the North American audience). Zápara dirigentes used translation as a vehicle for exploiting the heightened symbolic power of an elder or community member speaking only in Kichwa or Zápara (Graham 2002:208–209). When the elders' speeches were translated into Spanish, the result was an appreciation of these messages as distinctively Indigenous because of the symbolism of the performance (Graham 2002:193).

In the role of translator, Zápara dirigentes made certain that elders did not have to speak publicly in Spanish but could speak in Kichwa and Zápara.

Although most of the elders were familiar with Spanish, they preferred not to speak it because few were fluent (especially the female elders, who generally understand some but do not speak). Yet, transferring a message accurately from one language to another was not as important as maintaining an imagined separation between Zápara and Kichwa on one side and Spanish on the other. In the case of Carlos, the elder introduced in chapter 2, preserving this distinction was at times difficult for Zápara dirigentes. Because he spent more than a decade outside the Zápara communities, Carlos knew Spanish quite well. He was one of the most fluent speakers of Spanish *and* Zápara, although Kichwa was his primary language.

As mentioned in chapter 2, Carlos was a living embodiment of the Záparas' hybrid linguistic history. However, he upset the problematic division that contemporary multicultural and plurinational discourses often construct between Indigenous languages such as Zápara and "Western" languages such as Spanish. Although Carlos's fluency in Zápara established him (and, by extension, his community) as authentic, his fluency in Spanish potentially damaged this legitimacy. The fact that he could speak directly to external audiences in Spanish also meant that dirigentes were less able to edit the content of what he said.

On my first trip to Jandiayacu in 2002, María warned me about talking too much to Carlos, saying that my time would be better spent conversing with elders who had spent less time outside the Zápara communities. She also criticized Carlos for being (in her estimation) the only elder who knew Spanish well. María was present for several of my conversations with Carlos, and she tried in vain to direct the form and content of his speech. On one occasion, she asked him to tell us some Zápara stories. When he began talking in Spanish about the 1941 border war, she interrupted him and told him to speak in *sápara shimi* ("Zápara language" in Kichwa). By opting to speak in Spanish, Carlos chose a grammatical code that did not sufficiently index Zápara-ness for María. Carlos complained that he was not feeling well and did not want to speak Zápara. María backed off and told Carlos that it was fine to speak in Spanish but that he should tell a story unique to the Zápara, not a *historia mestiza* (mestizo story). She complained that his rendition of the border war was more about Ecuador than about the Zápara. Instead, she wanted him to tell a story about Tsitsano, a creation figure unique to the Zápara oral tradition (see Ushigua 2006). Carlos agreed, but instead of telling a story about Tsitsano, he told one about a blood-sucking monster who had terrorized the Zápara in mythological times. He introduced it by saying in Spanish, "Antes que había, no sé, un diablo. Creo que era un diablo [Long ago there was, I don't know, a devil. I think that's what it was, a devil]." María quickly corrected Carlos, saying in Spanish, "¡Espírito malo!

¡Espírito malo! [Evil spirit! Evil spirit!]" Carlos, looking annoyed, repeated "Espírito malo" and continued with his tale. The problem, as María later explained, was that "devil" is a Western Christian concept, not a Zápara one.

This interaction was obviously driven by my presence as a non-Zápara interlocutor. However, it does illustrate a broader dynamic at work in Zápara dirigentes' attempts to frame elders' linguistic performances in a way that fit neatly into dominant perceptions of Indigenous cultural purity. Most dirigentes were more cautious in their appraisal of Carlos than of the other elders. Throughout my research, Zápara dirigentes never asked him to speak publicly on the few occasions he was in Puyo to see a doctor, the way they had with some of the other elders. However, he was included in video and print media that NAZAE produced—instances in which dirigentes were able to more readily shape his language and message.

Family and gender politics were also at play in the dirigentes' treatment of Carlos. At the time of my research, all the core dirigentes were from the same nuclear family and community. Most were related to Carlos, either as nephews or nieces, as he was the head of a different nuclear family from a different community. Additionally, in public performances, dirigentes usually chose to forefront one of the two female elders from their community instead of Carlos, presumably because of his gender. Within widely circulating discourses of Indigeneity and environmentalism, Indigenous women have been particularly distinguished as nurturers of "traditional" knowledge and protectors of "Mother Earth" (Muratorio 1998:410–411). Throughout my ethnographic research on NAZAE, the trope of women as the proverbial "keepers of the culture torch" surfaced often in Zápara political rhetoric as an indication of the "purity" and continuity of Zápara culture. NAZAE leaders often privileged female elders as public symbols of the preservation of language, culture, and the Záparas' rain forest environs. In short, dirigentes combined—intentionally or not—Carlos's position in family networks and gender discourses with his multilingualism to deem him a somewhat inappropriate symbol of Zápara cultural and linguistic purity (Rappaport 2005:41).

Graham (2002:183, 211) describes strategies like the ones discussed above—combining languages, employing visual symbols of Indigenous culture, using translation—as creative adaptations "typical of native Amazonians' practice." These are, in her estimation, strategies through which Indigenous spokespeople further their goals and causes by framing them "in terms that appeal to Western values" (Conklin and Graham 1995:704). However, as the examples in this section suggest, Zápara self-representation was not just about creating symbols that resonated with external audiences. Rather, it was part of a process whereby Zápara dirigentes actively redefined which combinations of linguistic knowledge and life history "counted" as valid representations of Zápara "tradition." They created new possibilities for the recognition of their communities by connecting them to larger political spheres, but they also reproduced significant aspects of dominant discourses of Indigeneity in the process. In their role as translators, for example, Zápara dirigentes reified the separation between legitimate Indigenous culture and language and the illegitimate use of Spanish.

Managing Authenticity

Ethnographer Suzanne Oakdale (2004:60) argues that anthropologists have given considerable attention to the ways in which Indigenous leaders have projected their identities outward but that less has been paid to how local identities have changed as a result of Indigenous peoples' participation in broader political struggles. In a discussion of Brazilian Kayabi representation, Oakdale (2004:61) observes that "although Kayabi individuals are developing notions of 'culture' and 'Indian ethnicity' in dialogue with non-Kayabi at various supra-local events, at the same time they are also engaged with fellow Kayabi." The result, she argues, is a dual process in which leaders publicly represent Kayabi identity in a manner that accords with national-level discourses of Indigenous culture and simultaneously put this refashioned identity "to use for their own locally specific purposes" (Oakdale 2004:61). Kayabi leaders play an important role in "tailoring" borrowed frameworks to fit local concepts and preexisting political structures.

Zápara dirigentes, like their Kayabi counterparts, not only shaped how Indigenous identity was represented to outsiders. They also engaged in the process of redefining what constituted local Zápara identity so that it fit within current multicultural and plurinational discourses. This was most apparent in their interactions with rival leaders from the Comuna Záparo (Záparo Commune). Zápara dirigentes' authority as leaders was tied to the imagined boundary between Indigenous and mestizo society and their ability to navigate it (Briggs 1996). One of the ways in which they reinforced their local authority was by establishing themselves on the side of "Indigenous society" and positioning rival Comuna Záparo leaders on the side of "national mestizo society." Zápara dirigentes repeatedly claimed that the Comuna Záparo leaders were illegitimate representatives of Zápara culture because they did not speak Zápara, were affiliated with missionaries, and were of mixed Indigenous/mestizo descent. Conversely, Zápara dirigentes emphasized the "purity"—constructed as a lack of exogamy and cultural contact—of their own communities' cultural practice.

Since NAZAE's creation, there has been tension between the Zápara dirigentes and the Comuna Záparo leaders over who can legitimately claim

Zápara identity. The advantage that the Zápara dirigentes had was that they made themselves synonymous with the Zápara language at the time when the idea of a revived Zápara identity gained regional and national political attention. UNESCO's recognition of the Zápara language drew publicity to NAZAE dirigentes, who were featured on the national evening news and on the front page of Ecuador's largest newspaper. Indeed, one of the primary ways Zápara dirigentes distinguished themselves from the Comuna Záparo leaders was through language. In October 2002 Bartolo explained to me that the term *Zápara* meant "People of the Forest." He said that the term *Zápara* was what speakers of the language used to refer to themselves and to the language.[3] Bartolo asserted that *Zápara* is the accepted term of reference for the language, and its speakers have insisted on its official use in press releases and government documents. However, *Zápara* was not the term that members of the Comuna Záparo used to refer to themselves, but *Záparo*—the only difference being the final vowel. "*Záparo*," Bartolo said, "is a type of basket."[4] That the Comuna Záparo leaders could not get the name of their own nationality right, he noted, indicated their illegitimacy as "real" Zápara—a sentiment echoed by other Zápara dirigentes throughout my field research.

In March 2003 I had a conversation with another NAZAE dirigente, Oswaldo, about the Comuna Záparo leaders' knowledge of the Zápara language. Oswaldo had been active in the Zápara nationality's organization since its inception. At the time, he was director of teacher training for the Zápara education program. In his estimation, the Comuna Záparo leaders had not lived "as Zápara" for a long time. He claimed that these leaders came from families and communities that welcomed Protestant missionaries. In contrast, Oswaldo said, the Zápara had always resisted missionaries, and this was a sign of their cultural integrity. In several publications and testimonies, Zápara dirigentes accused missionaries of being agents of cultural assimilation (see, for example, *El Comercio* 2001; NAZAE 2001b). For example, Bartolo was quoted in a newspaper article as saying, "Because we want to preserve our traditions, the missionaries and priests have not helped us" (Hoy 1999). For these reasons, Oswaldo explained, the Comuna Záparo leaders could not speak Zápara and should not identify as Zápara.

The Zápara bundled the Comuna Záparo leaders' apparent lack of Zápara mastery with other markers of cultural inauthenticity to "prove" their illegitimacy. Oswaldo emphasized the Comuna Záparo's ties to the Asociación de Indígenas Evangélicos de Pastaza (AIEPRA) to highlight what he saw as a significant political distinction between them and NAZAE. Unlike the Comuna Záparo, he stressed, NAZAE had been recognized by "real" Indigenous organizations, such as OPIP, CONFENIAE, and CONAIE.

Organizations like OPIP and CONFENIAE and their member communities have consistently petitioned the Ecuadorian state for Indigenous language education and Indigenous land rights and have opposed environmentally destructive oil extraction in the Ecuadorian Amazon. In contrast, Oswaldo noted matter-of-factly, evangelical Indigenous organizations and communities have embraced capitalist development and oil extraction and have looked forward to being integrated into the national economy. In Oswaldo's view, evangelical organizations like AIEPRA and organizations like the Comuna Záparo opposed "true" Indigenous political goals—a further indication of their illegitimacy.

In April 2003 I had a similar conversation with María, who underscored how the Comuna Záparo leaders' political views, as well as their cultural background, made them invalid representatives of the Zápara nationality. She spent most of the time talking about OPIP's 1992 Marcha Indígena por la Vida (Indigenous March for Life), when Indigenous people walked from Puyo to Quito with the goal of pressuring the Ecuadorian government to recognize Indigenous land tenure in Pastaza province (Sawyer 1997; Whitten, Whitten, and Chango 1997). María and two of her brothers participated in the march, walking approximately 150 miles to the national capital (figure 3.2). She claimed that the Comuna Záparo leaders and other "evangelical Indians" harassed the marchers. "The evangelicals," she said, "got together to oppose the march. They showed up with the police and threw rocks at us." According to Maria, OPIP and its constituents successfully reached Quito only because "most of the Indigenous people were with OPIP."

María described an interaction she had with the president of the Comuna Záparo after the OPIP march and the Ecuadorian government's titling of the Bloque Záparo in 1993.[5] She said that the Comuna Záparo's president had taunted her, saying that he had a Zápara territory but she did not. She replied, "Do you know what, pal? [This] territory is not just yours. We are Záparas. We have the right to this territory. You are not Zápara." When the Comuna Záparo president asked María why she was sure that he was not Zápara, María told me, she responded, "Your grandfather is mestizo. Your great-grandfather was Zápara. But you're mestizo." María told me that after this exchange she traveled to Peru to visit with Zápara elders who lived on the Tigre River, northwest of the city of Iquitos. The elders told María, "The person who is criticizing you is not Zápara. He is mestizo."

In our conversation, María evoked notions of purity as a way of discrediting the Comuna Záparo organization and its leaders. She constructed an arbitrary division based on an idealized, all-or-nothing Indigenous versus non-Indigenous dichotomy, placing herself and her fellow dirigentes on the side of "true" Zápara. She highlighted particular aspects of the Comuna

Figure 3.2 Zápara activists participating in a 2003 parade in downtown Puyo with other nationalities and community organizations. Photo by author.

Záparo leaders' personal histories and practices as departures from Indigenous ways of doing things—opposition to "legitimate" Indigenous politics, land theft, mestizo ancestry.

María spoke in Spanish throughout most of our conversation while criticizing other Indigenous leaders for being mestizo and not speaking an Indigenous language. By speaking in Spanish, María risked these same criticisms. In order to avoid being perceived as "too fluent" in Spanish, María began our conversation in Kichwa but switched to Spanish to tell me the story of the march—in her words, to make sure that I understood everything. By initiating our conversation in Kichwa, María used the authenticity of the language to index the message she was about to deliver in Spanish as legitimately Indigenous. Furthermore, in citing my presence and language abilities (or, more accurately, deficiencies) as her reason for using Spanish, María asserted that the use of Spanish was not her "normal" or preferred channel for communication. Additionally, while speaking in Spanish, María drew from narratives of traditionalism, language preservation, cultural death, and incursion to convey herself and her message as authentic in juxtaposition to the Comuna Záparo leaders.

Conclusion

My concern in this chapter is to show the challenges that the "contradictory terrain" of emergent multicultural discourses has produced for Zápara leaders and their communities (Hale 2006:114, drawing on Clifford 2000). Zápara dirigentes adopted a range of creative strategies to present a consistent and coherent identity as a nationality in order to advance their political goals. These dirigentes' representation of Zápara culture relied upon establishing seemingly close "links" between contemporary Zápara and precontact "authentic bearers of tradition" (Briggs 1996:449,459–461). NAZAE dirigentes' authority was grounded on their ability to mitigate the "distance" between idealized representations of identity and on-the-ground practice when referring to their own communities (Briggs 1996:459–461). Simultaneously, they emphasized this distance when talking about the practice of rival Zápara leaders, pointing out the "gaps" between the Comuna Záparo leaders' present and past practices as means to question their authority.

Previous anthropological studies of Indigenous self-representation have critiqued Indigenous leaders' deployment of essentialist images of Indigenous culture in interethnic encounters like the ones described in this chapter (Conklin 1997; Jackson 1991; Ramos 1998).[6] Anthropologist Charles Hale (2006) argues, however, that such a critique undermines local political struggles while overlooking state requirements for recognition and special rights that often privilege essentialist representations of Indigenous culture (see also Briggs 1996; Cepek 2008; Clifford 2000).

In the same vein, ethnographer Joanne Rappaport (2005:37) proposes that academics "inquire into the specificities" of particular local contexts to understand why Indigenous activists engage in essentialist discourses, whether they see these discourses as "appropriate political strategies for fostering pluralism," and whether they believe that "these discourses are essentialist at all." According to Rappaport, the Colombian Nasa activists and intellectuals she studied do not view themselves as stereotyping Indigenous culture but as activating cultural difference in order to further their communities' autonomy. Rather than see culture as a "concrete and preexisting thing," Rappaport (2005:38–39) argues, these activists envision it as more of a "political utopia"—a tool they can use as a guide for future political action, the reconstruction of alternative life ways, and the creation of an "ethnic polity protected from the hegemonic forces that surround them." She also notes that Indigenous languages and shamanic practices have been useful for demarcating Nasa difference from dominant Colombian society as well as encouraging a discourse of ethnic revival within local communities (Rappaport 2005:39). Finally, Rappaport (2005:39–40) asserts that Nasa activists have engaged the essentialist stereotypes attributed to them by dominant Colombian society, employing them to "force their listeners to rethink once dominant ethnic categories."

However, when Rappaport's approach to Indigenous representation in Colombia is applied to the Zápara, it falls short in explaining the complex power dynamics at work in Indigenous leaders' practice. Her emphasis on the voices and rationale of local Indigenous activists is important. It demonstrates that they are critically adapting multicultural discourses to their own ends. Yet, privileging local actors' accounts of their political activity belies the potential role these actors may also play in reproducing aspects of dominant discourses and power relations.

As demonstrated in this chapter, Zápara dirigentes have adopted dominant discourses of Indigenous tradition and cultural difference in their effort to achieve external recognition and internal unification. They do not regard these discourses as essentialist but, in keeping with their Nasa counterparts, as important means for revalorizing aspects of Zápara culture and identity. Nor have they engaged in a wholesale adoption of these discourses. In certain regards, they have refashioned dominant concepts of Indigenous culture to conform to local meanings and discourses. Nevertheless, Zápara dirigentes continue to articulate their concerns through dominant categories. Although they undoubtedly contest and expand certain aspects of these, through the process of self-representation they also reinforce dominant notions of authenticity, particularly in their interactions with Comuna Záparo leaders. I return to this issue in the book's conclusion, in which I demonstrate the fractious impact this has had on the Zápara nationality, eroding a potential base for pan-Zápara political action. I now turn to an examination of similar tensions between Zápara dirigentes and their constituents over the content and practice of community bilingual education.

4 The Paradoxes of Intercultural Education

Every May, Puyo celebrates its "founding" by Dominican friars with a festival that includes a carnival with rides, a traveling zoo, cotton candy, and heavy drinking. One of the central events is a beauty contest in which local young women compete for the title of Reina de Puyo (Queen of Puyo). The pageant lasts several hours and unfolds in Miss America style—the candidates perform dance routines, give speeches, model swimsuits and evening gowns, and do individual performances. When I attended in 2003, spectators who were unable to get a seat inside Puyo's civic auditorium viewed MTV-inspired videos of the candidates on several large-screen televisions facing the street. The woman chosen as the Reina de Puyo gains a degree of local celebrity status because she heads a large parade that signals the end of the festivities.

Across town from the auditorium where the Reina de Puyo contest takes place is the Dirección de Educación Bilingüe de Pastaza (Administration of Bilingual Education in Pastaza), which coordinates Indigenous education in the province. Each year, the dirección hosts a parallel celebration of Indigenous culture during the Puyo festival. Indigenous organizations erect booths on the dirección's grounds to sell crafts and food. There is a night of games in which individuals from various nationalities compete in activities such as spear throwing, chicha (beer) drinking, and blowgun shooting. The dirección's activities serve as a reminder of Indigenous peoples' presence in the area before the "official" (Hispanic) establishment of Puyo.

On the morning of May 9, 2003, the Indigenous festivities moved to the civic auditorium, where a fair-skinned mestiza had been crowned Reina de Puyo the night before. Another contest was set to take place on that day. This one, coordinated by the dirección, determined who would be the year's

Figure 4.1 Contestant in the Princesa Indígena de Pastaza pageant. Photo by author.

Princesa Indígena de Pastaza (Indigenous Princess of Pastaza). Gradually, the bleachers on both sides of the auditorium filled with spectators who were informally grouped by nationality. The Reina de Puyo also attended, along with the contest's judges: a reporter, a city official, and a police officer. Eventually, the candidates themselves, young women between seventeen and twenty-three years old, arrived on stage. The princesas wore feather-and-fur bikini versions of their nationalities' "traditional" dress and were accompanied by bare-chested male *guerreros* (warriors) with spears (figure 4.1).[1] Much of the talk and imagery of the pageant centered on tropes of "defending" Indigenous languages as the vessels of cultural tradition and identity.

Each Indigenous nationality in Pastaza—Kichwa, Shuar, Zápara, Achuar, Shiwiar, and Waorani—had a candidate. The first, from the Kichwa nationality, addressed the audience in Kichwa and Spanish, discussing her community's proud history and contemporary political struggles. A Shuar candidate followed, and then the Zápara, a young woman named Elena. I sat with roughly a dozen Zápara, and together we cheered for her. The Zápara were proud that Elena was in the pageant—the year before was the first time a Zápara representative had participated in the contest. In the days before the pageant, many of them helped Elena to make her dress and practice her performance routine.

Elena was not worried about her dress, her dancing, or her performance, though. She was worried about the short speech she had to give in Zápara—a language she did not speak. Elena grew up in Puyo and speaks fluent Kichwa and Spanish. Her mother is Zápara, and her grandmother is a Zápara speaker. Her father, Oswaldo, is Kichwa but worked for NAZAE, first as a community instructor and then as a curriculum specialist. According to the rules set by the dirección, Elena had to give a speech in Zápara. The princesas were graded on their eloquence, the political message of their speech, their dress, their dance, and their mock performance of agricultural work. Additionally, each candidate had to address the audience in her "maternal" language and then self-translate into Spanish. The day before the pageant, Elena had asked her aunt, who knew some Zápara, to write her speech. Although she had practiced the night before, on the day of the contest she was too nervous to recite it from memory—she was the only candidate who used a note card while addressing the audience in her nationality's language. When she finished, the audience clapped, and the announcer, a dirección staffer, offered words of encouragement and explained to the audience that the Zápara were engaged in the difficult process of reviving their national language.

Elena's participation in the Princesa Indígena contest not only highlighted the challenges the Zápara faced in revitalizing their language but also revealed some of the general issues surrounding Indigenous education in Ecuador. The dirección's contest stressed the importance of fluency in Indigenous languages for delineating distinct identities, while positioning Spanish as a necessary vehicle for cross-cultural communication in Puyo's urban space.

Indigenous activists throughout South America have emphasized bilingual education as a means of encouraging the official integration of Indigenous peoples within their respective nation-states. In a study of Peruvian education, anthropologist María Elena García nicely sums up the importance of bilingual education for promoting interculturalism:

> Multiculturalism is the recognition of a reality (Peru is a country of diverse cultural and linguistic makeup); interculturalidad [interculturalism] is the *practice* of a multiculturalism in which citizens reach across cultural and linguistic differences to imagine a democratic community. In that vein, bilingual intercultural education is the mechanism par excellence used to foster intercultural unity out of multicultural difference. (García 2005:3)

García (2005:109) remarks, however, that in Peru there remains a gap between official discourses of inclusion and recognition of multiculturalism and the state's persistent underfunding of intercultural education, which has perpetuated Indigenous peoples' exclusion.

As I demonstrate in this chapter, activists in Ecuador have confronted this same issue in their implementation of Indigenous education. Furthering intercultural education has been a significant step towards realizing CONAIE's goal of creating a plurinational state (Pallares 2002:203). Moreover, Indigenous education reform has been particularly important in providing administrative training and knowledge of state bureaucracy to local organizations such as NAZAE. However, the secondary position of the Princesa Indígena contest to the Reina de Puyo pageant hints at the continued marginalization of Indigenous languages. Bilingual, intercultural education is supposed to make Indigenous students literate in their own languages *and* competent in Spanish. Yet, this is rarely the case in poorly funded Indigenous schools. A recent report notes that, in parts of Ecuador, per capita government expenditures for non-Indigenous students are twice those for Indigenous students (*El Comercio* 2008e).

In this chapter, I show the impact of NAZAE's taking over the administration of Zápara education—a process that strengthened the organization and opened up an important avenue for furthering the revalorization of Zápara language and identity. However, given the paucity of government money for education, Zápara community schools have remained resource poor and are staffed with instructors who are not sufficiently trained and who lack the requisite linguistic skills to implement multilingual programs. Students in the Zápara communities have not received an education that gives them literacy and fluency in Spanish, Kichwa, and Zápara. As I demonstrate at the end of this chapter, this has produced some friction between NAZAE activists and community residents, who feel that ongoing problems with community schooling are an indication that they and their children are not benefiting equally from Zápara self-organization.

Education and Identity

Throughout Latin America, schools have been important spaces for reinforcing and contesting dominant regimes of citizenship and political participation (Luykx 1999; see also Gustafson 2002; Hornberger 1997, 2000). Anthropologist Fiona Wilson (2001:313) argues that in rural Peru "the school has taken over the functions of the military outpost," because it is the primary rural institution in which state symbols are shown and students are "taught to be citizens" through bodily practices such as saluting the flag and marching. As part of agrarian reform programs in the mid-twentieth century, governments in Bolivia, Ecuador, and Peru targeted rural schools as important sites for converting highland *Indios* (Indians) into Spanish-speaking *campesinos* (peasants) (Hornberger 2000; Wilson 2001:324). Unsurprisingly, Indigenous activists in Ecuador have focused on rural schools as sites for contesting prior models of citizenship based on linguistic and cultural assimilation.

Throughout Ecuador's history, elites denied Indigenous peoples access to Spanish-language education as a way of reinforcing their subordinate status. In the latter half of the sixteenth century and early part of the seventeenth, Franciscan and Jesuit priests founded schools in Quito to educate the children of Spanish conquistadors. A few schools were also created to educate the city's Indigenous people, but these differed from the schools for Spanish descendents in their approaches to curriculum and instruction. Spanish missionaries considered Indigenous people to be subhumans who were incapable of abstract thought and could learn things only through imitation (Yánez Cossío 1995:15). During this period, priests wrote early grammars and dictionaries of Kichwa. However, these texts were not intended for teaching Indigenous people, but for friars and priests to use in evangelizing them (Yánez Cossío 1995:13).

The situation of Indigenous education did not change after Ecuador gained its independence from Spain. Throughout much of the nineteenth century, the country was ruled by conservative elites who sought to maintain strict control of Indigenous labor (Larson 2004:120). Literacy was a requisite for voting in the new republic (and remained so until 1978), so denying Indigenous people schooling in Spanish was an effective means of excluding them from full participation in national society and politics. According to historian Erin O'Connor (2007), from time to time, elite politicians decried the "miserable" conditions of Indigenous laborers in the country and promised schooling to help raise Indigenous people out of their "wretched" state. For example, O'Connor (2007:65) notes that in 1869 conservative president Gabriel García Moreno (1861–1865, 1869–1875) declared the need to build primary schools in rural areas. Through elite-mandated schooling, he reasoned, Indigenous peoples could be stripped of their laziness, ignorance, and duplicity and would further Ecuador's economic progress by serving as the country's diligent labor force (Larson 2004:119; O'Connor 2007:64–65).

In 1895 Ecuador's liberal coastal elites rebelled against highland conservatives and declared General Eloy Aflaro president of the country. Ecuador's coastal economy was based on the export of cocoa, but, given the region's "relatively scarce population," plantation owners were constantly short of labor (Clark 2005:55). Elites in Guayaquil sought to rectify this by freeing highland Indigenous people from peonage, thus enabling them to leave highland estates and migrate to the coast, where they could sell their labor to plantation owners (Crain 1990:45). To this end, the liberal government instituted measures to protect the rights of Indigenous laborers and established official channels through which Indigenous people could take complaints to the government (Clark 2005:55; see also Clark 1994; Guerrero 1997). In its new role as a "protector" of Indigenous peoples, the liberal government proposed education reforms that would help Indigenous peoples to become free laborers in a modern economy.

Historian Marc Becker (2003:136) notes that liberals saw education for Indigenous people as an important tool for subverting the power of conservative landlords, who feared that better educated, literate workers "would be harder to cheat and exploit." However, Becker notes that Indigenous parents were not keen on the idea of elite-imposed education, which was designed without their input and retained notions of Indigenous racial inferiority. Indeed, liberals' concern "for the education of Indians revolved around a desire to improve their hygiene, train them in new agricultural techniques, and raise their cultural horizons" (Becker 2003:136). Given this, parents in highland communities such as Salasaca would not send their children to the local school because of the instructors' "attempts to eradicate 'paganism' and insistence that students have short hair, shoes, and European/ North American dress" (Wogan 2004:64).

Becker (2003:136–137) argues that most Indigenous people were interested in obtaining education for themselves or their children but wanted schooling that was developed with their interests and cultural beliefs in mind. In the 1940s the first Indigenous-run schools emerged in Cayambe in response to grassroots demands for improved Indigenous education. As Becker notes, these schools were distinct in that they were initiated by Indigenous women activists in collaboration with urban white women. Also, the instructors were Indigenous people who taught in Kichwa. The schools were so successful and "posed such a threat to elite hegemony that in the 1950s and 1960s the government attempted to replace them with [its] own" (Becker 2003:137).

Although some Andean missions instituted programs similar to the Cayambe schools, bilingual education in highland Ecuador was not widespread until the 1960s, when the state instituted rural literacy and education programs as a component of its agrarian reforms. These programs received little support in Indigenous communities, which saw them as representing the desires of Ecuador's oligarchy and not of its Indigenous citizens (Becker 2003:137). Moreover, education for Indigenous people was spotty, and for those who did learn some Spanish, the language was not a magic key to inclusion. Instead of being marginalized as Kichwa speakers, Indigenous peasants were deemed inferior for their rurally inflected variant of Spanish (see Gustafson 2002:275).

In lowland Ecuador, evangelical and Catholic missionaries were the main providers of Indigenous education until the 1980s. During the nineteenth century, Jesuit priests created mission schools for "children of both sexes" with the misguided purpose of eradicating the "ignorance and barbarism" they saw in the region (Pierre 1988[1889]:266). At the beginning of the twentieth century, Josephine and Salesian (and, to a lesser extent, Dominican) missionaries emphasized Spanish as a means for Indigenous people to access "the mestizo world and the capitalist economy" and free themselves from debt peonage (Muratorio 1991:165). Some missionaries adopted extreme measures in their efforts to accomplish this goal. The Salesians forced Shuar children to attend boarding schools where they were separated from their families and subjected to Christian indoctrination (Rubenstein 2002:103–105).[2] Not all missionaries imposed boarding schools on Indigenous communities in the Ecuadorian Amazon, however. Beginning in the mid-twentieth century, Protestant missionaries worked with Indigenous communities to establish bilingual day schools (A.-C. Taylor 1981:659; see also Rival 2002:161). Though decidedly paternalistic in approach, Protestant schools tended to valorize Indigenous languages more than did Catholic mission schools.

Beginning in the 1970s, Indigenous activists in the Amazon and the Andes initiated their own bilingual education programs. The Shuar instituted a program to teach parents and children through radio programming. The Shuar Federation's Escuelas Radiofónicas (Radio Schools) made it possible for students to obtain literacy in both languages without leaving home. Likewise, literacy programs emerged in the highlands that stressed the maintenance of Indigenous languages and challenged prior models of state assimilation (Moya 1990:338). Highland Indigenous peoples founded a number of these programs with the help of Catholic institutions that shifted their efforts, from conversion to Indigenous rights and cultural preservation, after Vatican II (Brysk 2004:27). For instance, self-administered Indigenous education programs emerged in the highland provinces of Bolivar in 1972 and Cotopaxi in 1977 (see Moya 1990:337).

Following Ecuador's transition from military to civilian rule in 1979 (see Isaacs 1993), the state funded several Indigenous-language literacy programs to create pedagogical materials in Kichwa and train Indigenous instructors (Moya 1990:333–336; Selverston-Scher 2001:86). However, government-sponsored programs maintained the idea that Indigenous peoples could experience the full benefits of citizenship only through linguistic and cultural assimilation (Crain 1990:48). These programs functioned as important spaces for young Indigenous leaders to network with other activists and learn more about state bureaucracies, but they did not afford Indigenous peoples much control over the content or direction of their education (Selverston-Scher 2001:88; Yashar 2005:141–142). In response, Indigenous leaders petitioned for Indigenous-administered bilingual education programs. For example, CONFENIAE started its own self-managed bilingual education program in the 1980s, the Proyecto Alternativo de Educación Bilingüe de la CONFENIAE (Alternative Project for Bilingual Education of CONFENIAE, or PAEBIC). In 1986 Indigenous leaders got a boost when the Federal Republic of Germany funded the Proyecto de Educación Bilingüe Intercultural (Project for Bilingual Intercultural Education, or PEBI) to work with Ecuador's Ministry of Education and Culture to promote Kichwa literacy (Abram 1992). In contrast to prior programs, PEBI stressed Kichwa as the primary language of instruction and treated Spanish "as a second language" (Moya 1990:337).

PEBI laid the groundwork for the Dirección Nacional de Educación Intercultural Bilingüe (National Administration of Bilingual Intercultural Education, or DINEIB)—an Indigenous-administered program created in 1989. President Rodrigo Borja (1988–1992) recognized the program as having the same status as the government-run education system and agreed to fully fund it (Moya 1990:340). However, DINEIB never received the entire $800,000 that Borja promised for setting up the administration—giving Indigenous education official recognition yet insufficient funds for its full implementation (Selverston-Scher 2001:63).

Nonetheless, DINEIB's creation increased the visibility of bilingual education in Ecuador and also the prominence and power of Ecuador's Indigenous movement. It created employment opportunities for Indigenous people as instructors in rural communities. Political scientist Melina Selverston-Scher (2001:88) argues that, by taking control of instructor hiring, DINEIB also challenged clientelism in Ecuador. National and provincial politicians controlled the hiring of teachers and used these positions to grant political favors in return for votes. Selverston-Scher (2001:88) notes that in Napo province the congressional representative named 80 percent of the instructors, with the provincial director of education and other officials controlling the rest. All this hiring power passed to CONAIE after DINEIB was created.

DINEIB's creation coincided with an increase in neoliberal economic reforms during the 1990s. Neoliberal discourses of decentralization and Indigenous demands for greater local autonomy paralleled each other on the subject of autonomous Indigenous education (Gustafson 2002:277, 280).

The World Bank emphasized education as an indispensable tool for enabling individuals and local communities to become capable self-providers (Gustafson 2002:277; World Bank 1995a). National Law No. 150, which was enacted on April 15, 1992, made DINEIB an "administratively and financially decentralized organization." The Ministry of Education and Culture's new Model for Intercultural Bilingual Education 1993 prioritized the maintenance of Indigenous languages and cultural practices in Indigenous education (see Yánez Cossío 1995:180–212). In contrast to prior models of education, which stressed the centrality of government curriculums, the 1993 model underscored the importance of locally specific Indigenous education and community control over the content of instruction.

Yet, structural adjustment programs entailed dramatic cuts in government spending, particularly on social services. Officials justified these cuts, claiming that they were necessary measures for generating revenue to pay Ecuador's ballooning foreign debts. Indigenous education was particularly affected by government cuts. President Durán Ballén (1992–1996) sought to "fix" Ecuador's economic situation by privatizing government services and diminishing "the size and functions of state agencies" (Treakle 1998:225). As one component of the latter, he proposed to dismantle DINEIB—a move that was halted by considerable Indigenous protest (Selverston-Scher 2001:89). Although DINEIB survived intact, overall funding for education slowed to a trickle during the 1990s, threatening the administration's mission (see Pallares 2002:204).

Ecuador's constitution was revised in 1998 to include Indigenous peoples' right to bilingual education. Most recently, Ecuador's 2008 constitution declared Spanish the official language of Ecuador and Spanish, Kichwa, and Shuar the official languages of "intercultural relation" (Article 2). But state recognition of Indigenous bilingualism has been accompanied by a general unwillingness to grant government funds for education reforms. Rather than improve the situation of Indigenous students, the state's official recognition of Indigenous languages has glossed over the persistence of a two-tiered education system in which Spanish-only education is privileged over bilingual education. Over the past decade, Ecuador has provided 10 percent less in funds for Indigenous students in primary education and 40 percent less for those in secondary education, compared with non-Indigenous students (Torres 2005:10; see also Ponce 2004). Given this considerable inequality in state financing, Indigenous education has often relied on whatever external funding it can obtain to try to supply communities with basic services (Torres 2005:24).

These disparities stem from the fact that government approval of Indigenous education within the Ecuadorian state has been anything but unanimous over the past two decades. Many traditional Ecuadorian elites continue to oppose Indigenous bilingual education because they claim that special Indigenous rights undermine the unity of the Ecuadorian state (Macdonald 2002:182; Sawyer 2004:206). President Borja's own Democratic Left Party privately threatened to shun him if he followed through on DINEIB's creation (Selverston-Scher 2001:88). President Gutiérrez (2003–2005) tried to take administration of Indigenous education away from DINEIB and place it under direct government control, presumably as a way of sapping CONAIE's political influence (Torres 2005:24).

In sum, education reform has a long history of contradictory results for Ecuador's Indigenous peoples. DINEIB's creation and the decentralization of Indigenous education have augmented CONAIE's power and increased the validity of language as a marker of Indigenous identity. However, chronic shortages in funding for Indigenous education have impeded the advancement of intercultural reform and maintained inequality in the status quo. Many community education programs struggle to buy books and to install electricity in schools, much less offer instruction in both an Indigenous language and Spanish that is comparable to what urban students receive.

Zápara Trilingual Education

On July 24, 2000, the Ministry of Education, Culture, Sports, and Recreation (MEC) recognized the Dirección de Educación de la Nacionalidad Zápara del Ecuador (Administration of Education for the Zápara Nationality of Ecuador, or DIENAZE) as the official administrator of Zápara education (Ministerial Accord No. 100). MEC allotted DIENAZE a $40,000 annual budget for paying its staff and instructors (a dozen people in total) and providing pedagogical materials and upkeep for the Zápara community schools. In the years after its creation, DIENAZE worked to develop a curriculum that incorporated aspects of Zápara material culture, gave instructors specific cultural and linguistic training, and unified geographically isolated communities as a nationality. Additionally, it strove to impart to its students "scientific and technological knowledge of the outside world" to strengthen the Zápara nationality by educating its future lawyers, leaders, teachers, and tourism agents.[3]

DIENAZE's first task was to develop a series of literacy workbooks for teaching students and their parents to read and write in Kichwa and Spanish. The most basic of these taught students to copy letters before progressing to spelling in Kichwa; the most advanced workbooks contained writing and reading exercises in Spanish. In addition to the Kichwa–Spanish workbooks, DIENAZE created several basic Kichwa–Zápara texts. The first was divided into two sections, one in Kichwa and the other in Zápara. In each section, vocabulary words appeared below pictures of the objects they signified. For example, the Zápara word *ichawka* was placed below a drawing of a toucan. Students were supposed to copy the word in Zápara and then color in the drawing to practice using a pencil and to learn Zápara vocabulary. The problem with DIENAZE's Zápara workbooks was that the information presented to students was lexical and the exercises were not progressively more difficult, making it impossible to gain advanced literacy in Zápara from the workbooks.[4]

All of DIENAZE's workbooks were illustrated with drawings that depicted houses like the ones in which most Zápara families live—with rivers, fish, and monkeys, people drinking chicha—and, in some cases, with photos of family members to illustrate concepts such as "young" and "old." These workbooks followed the Freirian approach to literacy advocated by DINEIB, in which school texts reflect students' experiences.[5] When students progressed to reading short passages in Spanish, DIENAZE's workbooks included selections about NAZAE's political goals. For example, DIENAZE's Spanish literacy workbook contained passages such as this: "Our best industry is not petroleum. Our best industry is ecological tourism." Another passage read: "We take care of our health with medicine from our own land. Western medicine is very expensive. Also, it does not cure all sicknesses. Medicine from white people cures some sicknesses but makes others worse." Passages from DIENAZE's literacy workbooks introduced students to discourses of Indigenous ecological stewardship, Indigenous peoples' rights as Ecuadorian citizens, and the importance of organizing as Zápara. The workbooks highlighted students' connections to a regional political territory through their relationship to the Zápara language. They also emphasized that the Zápara language was a concrete link between Zápara culture and rain forest ecology.

Much of DIENAZE's education program was concerned with reinforcing the idea of a Zápara national territory, at the heart of which were community schools. The first of these schools was built in Llanchamacocha in the early 1990s. In 2003 DIENAZE built another school in Mazaramu with a grant from MEC. In meetings I attended and conversations I had with DIENAZE staff, Zápara dirigentes repeatedly emphasized the importance of these schools for reviving the Zápara language and teaching Zápara students about their rights as Ecuadorian citizens. Zápara schools were also centers for community gatherings and the storage of communal resources. In Llanchamacocha, the school building was the only place in the community with electricity. In 2002 the Zápara obtained support for a project to install a solar-powered generator in the building, along with outlets for light bulbs and plugs. Then children could play in the lit schoolhouse at night and listen to the radio—something that had required expensive batteries before. Additionally, adults gathered in the schools to discuss issues and problems that the community faced and how to best address them, such as what to do with a schoolteacher whom the community disliked.

The fact that most individuals passed through the schoolhouse on a regular basis made it an ideal site for circulating narratives of Zápara identity and citizenship. DIENAZE staff provided each of the schools with symbols of Zápara political culture, such as a map of the nationality's territory and pictures of its leaders. The staff also made posters about the Zápara language; the most common was a picture of a naked man and woman, with their body parts labeled in Zápara. Other aspects of Zápara material culture often adorned the schools; samples of Zápara pottery, baskets, and weaving, as well as dugout canoes and blowguns, hung from the ceiling of each school. These symbols, one of the DIENAZE representatives told me, brought the community and the rain forest into the classroom and made them more familiar to students.

Representations of Ecuadorian nationalism and the state were also prominent in Zápara schools. The Ecuadorian government and, more specifically, its Ministry of Education and Culture require that all school children revere the Ecuadorian nation. DIENAZE did not resist but instead embraced these practices: maps of the Zápara communities employed the Ecuadorian flag as the cartographic key for the school; an Ecuadorian flag was raised outside each of the schools at the beginning of the day; and at the head of the classroom was a placard with the Ecuadorian flag, along with a map of Ecuador and the national creed written in Spanish. Oswaldo, an instructor who created Zápara curriculum and trained teachers, explained to me that it was imperative that the students and the communities realize they are part of Ecuador. The state historically marginalized Indigenous peoples, denying them membership in the nation as long as they spoke Indigenous languages. It was key, he said, to teach students and communities that, as Indigenous peoples, they should be recognized as full citizens without having to deny their Zápara identity.

A central aspect of DIENAZE's education program included training schoolteachers in alternative pedagogical methods and educating them about NAZAE's goals and objectives, the history of the Zápara nationality, and the Zápara language. Twice a year, DIENAZE ran mandatory two-week training workshops in Puyo. I observed and participated in one of these workshops in April 2003. The training sessions began each morning around nine or nine-thirty and ended at noon, when the staff and instructors left to eat lunch and take a break from the midday humidity. All returned around three, fanning themselves and occasionally wiping the accumulating sweat off their brows and necks until the afternoon training session ended at five. During one of the sessions I attended, instructors were educated about methods and exercises for teaching Kichwa. They also watched a video filmed in an Indigenous school in the Ecuadorian Andes that emphasized the importance of experience-based learning. When the video was over, Diego, the DIENAZE director at the time, spoke to the instructors about experience-based education. He reminded the instructors that their students should always be doing something and stressed that each student should be treated as an individual and not be compared with other students. Diego's approach to education highlighted the need for each student to work at his or her own pace. He was explicit in stating that prior models of pedagogy, which relied on physical punishment to maintain classroom discipline, were not acceptable. The instructor should be an advocate for the students, he said, not an authority figure asserting his or her power through discipline.

Oswaldo followed Diego. He talked to the instructors about developing pedagogical materials for the schools. The problem, Oswaldo said, was that DIENAZE had little money to buy formal teaching materials. The solution was to create materials from the rain forest. By doing so, instructors could make the reality of the classroom more similar to the lived reality of the students. Oswaldo showed the instructors how to use various seeds and shells to develop counting games for teaching mathematics, such as the *taptana*. He claimed that the taptana was an Indigenous calculator, developed by the Inka for addition, subtraction, and record keeping. Each of the holes on the taptana represented a particular numerical value, which was marked by a wooden peg, much in the same manner that an abacus uses beads as numerical placeholders.

The following day, Oswaldo led a seminar on Zápara history and language. The seminar, which lasted for almost two days, focused on one of DIENAZE's Spanish literacy workbooks. The first section of the workbook narrated NAZAE's founding and discussed the Záparas' struggle to save their language, establish an autonomous territory, and provide basic services to their communities. At the end of the first part of the seminar, the teachers wrote down NAZAE's objectives, in addition to composing a short paragraph about what they would do to help save the Zápara language. The second section of the workbook expounded on the link between the Zápara language and Ecuador's rain forest ecology. This connection, the workbook claimed, was proven by the fact that the Zápara language has words to refer to all the plant and animal species one encounters in the rain forest. After discussing the Zápara language and its connection to the rain forest, Oswaldo asked the instructors to repeat the principal argument for UNESCO's recognition of the Zápara language. He also requested that they draw a map of Ecuador and locate the Zápara on it. Following these exercises, Oswaldo talked the instructors through the third part of the workbook, on Zápara phonology and vocabulary. He practiced the pronunciation of Zápara words with them and ended the session with a Zápara myth about boa constrictors. After the instructors read the myth together, Oswaldo asked them to gather in pairs and talk about the moral of the story. He then asked each instructor to tell a myth from his or her own nationality.

These activities were meant to give instructors an understanding of Zápara identity and reinforce participatory teaching methods. The last activity—each instructor telling a myth from his or her community—encouraged the instructors to take stock of their own knowledge. DIENAZE staff used this and other exercises to encourage the instructors themselves to become students and see what it is like to learn through hands-on practice and group problem-solving. Despite these efforts, a measurable gap remained between DIENAZE's goal of implementing participation-based education and what instructors actually did after they got to their community schools.

Community Education

Schooldays in the Zápara communities began with students gathering outside the school on the playing field or airstrip. The teacher arranged the children by height and gender, with the tallest boy at the head of the line and the shortest girl at the end. The students would then run a lap around the playing field before doing exercises. The teacher would raise the Ecuadorian flag, and, after saluting it, the students would enter the school. Once inside, the students were expected to recite a short greeting in Spanish, although most instruction was in Kichwa—the primary language of both the students and the instructors.

In conversations I had with Oswaldo about language education in the Zápara communities, he often said that it is important for students to study Zápara to get a better understanding of who they are. Yet, he always stressed that it is equally important that Zápara children learn Spanish without a Kichwa accent—something that would allow them greater mobility in Ecuador's education system and economy. The problem, though, was that the community instructors were not fluent in Spanish, nor did most of them have advanced literacy skills, making it unlikely that they could give students any meaningful spoken or written instruction in Spanish. Instructors taught students to repeat stock sayings in Spanish about Ecuador's history or about how students should behave, but never did they teach the students how to produce real conversation in the language. A significant portion of the students' time was spent copying sentences from the few antiquated books that were available in each of the schools, rather than actively exploring the issues surrounding Indigenous citizenship, as DIENAZE administrators had hoped. In short, DIENAZE's experience-based methods almost never made it from the workshops to the classrooms.

Although these workshops were a good start, two weeks was simply not enough to train instructors in alternative pedagogy. Wilson (2001:318–319) argues that as official discourses travel from the urban center to the rural periphery, they undergo a process of "translation" that the state cannot control, enabling rural schools to function as sites for challenging state inequality, injustice, and control. The same is also true for intercultural discourses that travel from the urban centers of Quito and Puyo to the rural Zápara communities through poorly equipped instructors. By the time an individual becomes an instructor, he or she has been through "a number of socializing experiences" (for example, teacher training) that can undermine intercultural discourses (Wilson 2001:319)—experiences that DIENAZE cannot mitigate with such limited training. Upon arrival in the community schools, instructors generally reverted to the drilling and memorization with which they were most familiar. According to government regulation, the instructors DIENAZE hired were required to have six years of secondary education and two years (it is now four) of training in an *instituto normal* (normal school), where the pedagogy stresses the maintenance of discipline and rote memorization (see Rival 2002:153, 164–165).

Another of DIENAZE's biggest problems was regular turnover in its instructors—the ones who were not kicked out by the communities left on their own after a year or less. If DIENAZE could not keep teachers in the first place, then it could not do much to improve their pedagogical and language skills over time. The instructors I met were from Kichwa communities in Napo and Pastaza provinces. Although the salary for rural instructors was low even when compared with the rest of Ecuador (about $125 per month), it was a good wage in rural Indigenous communities, where opportunities for other professional work were nonexistent. Yet, few of these instructors wanted to be away from their families in the relatively remote Zápara communities. In the end, most took jobs with DIENAZE until they could find work in a more desirable school.

In August 2004 I spoke with one of these instructors, Pilar. Upon finishing normal school, she hoped to return to her home community of Pacayacu as an instructor. However, no positions were open in Pacayacu's school, so she had taken a job with DIENAZE in Jandiayacu.

Pacayacu is considerably larger than any of the Zápara communities. Located on the upper Bobonaza River, it is also closer to Puyo and has had a more prolonged history of interaction with the region's economic center. Pilar was from what she described as a Christian family. They had a small plot of land where they grew food for their own subsistence as well as surplus for sale in Puyo. Her father spent much of his life working as a laborer in and around Puyo. In Pilar's eyes, he had worked hard to earn money for his family, and she was trying to follow his lead. Pilar's two children lived in Pacayacu with her parents. She wanted to leave Jandiayacu but said that the money she made working there was important for her family—she used it to make improvements on her house and buy her children new clothes. In comparison, she criticized the people in Jandiayacu who did not work to produce extra crops for sale (although she also complained of how isolated the community was and how difficult and expensive it was to get to Puyo).[6] Compounding Pilar's distaste for what she perceived as lack of "Christian" work ethic in Jandiayacu was her feeling that her authority as an instructor threatened male community leaders.

These tensions were apparent at an event I attended in 2004 to celebrate the closing of Jandiayacu's school for summer vacation. Around 10 a.m., parents trickled into the school and sat at the small desks and chairs while Pilar and the students waited at the front of the classroom. After most of the parents had arrived, Pilar thanked the community for its support and talked about how well the students had done that semester. She led everyone in saluting the Ecuadorian flag and recited the national creed in Spanish. The students, ranging in age from six to thirteen, then sang in small groups divided by grade and recited poems they had memorized in Spanish, Kichwa, and Zápara. Throughout the ceremony, parents heckled Pilar and tried to distract her. Several men raised their hands and mockingly called, "Profesora, Profesora," as though they were students asking permission to speak. When she looked at one of them, he looked away and started to laugh.

After the ceremony, Pilar did an inventory of the school's materials in front of everyone. She counted all the jars of paint, brushes, and books and then had Jandiayacu's *akameno* (a kind of mayor) verify the tally before locking everything in a makeshift closet. She then scolded the children and parents for stealing paint and paper from the school and using up these supplies. The following day, when we traveled out of the community together, Pilar explained that she could not teach without those materials. That the parents and children took things from the school was another indicator of their poor character in Pilar's opinion. "They are *mala gente* [bad people]," she lamented.

Community Dynamics

Parents often faulted instructors like Pilar for blaming them and their children for shortcomings in community education. DIENAZE hired the instructors, but parents had the final say in how long they stayed. In September 2002 I sat in on a community meeting in Llanchamacocha in which residents discussed the removal of their school's instructor. In the evening, male leaders from the community ambled from their houses across the grassy soccer field to the one-room schoolhouse. Assembled in the hot building, they voiced their opinions about renewing the current instructor. One man whose oldest children were students in the school was the first to speak up. He told everyone that he thought the instructor in question was good and was doing a passable job of teaching the children. The rest of the assembled group, however, opposed keeping the instructor. One commented that the instructor was from Napo province and spoke a strong dialect of Kichwa that differed from Pastaza Kichwa. The children could not easily understand the instructor and were suffering because of it. That year, the instructor in question was removed from Llanchamacocha's school and replaced with another instructor, who left after only a short time in the community.

Several factors informed the often shaky relationship between instructor and residents in the Zápara communities. Local gender politics was one. As I mention in chapter 3, positions of political authority are generally male-based in the Zápara communities, creating tension between male heads of households and female instructors like Pilar. Moreover, interethnic rivalry perhaps played a role in instructor–parent tensions. During my research, all the DIENAZE instructors were Napo or Pastaza Kichwa. Some Zápara from the Conambo River are married to Kichwa, but many thought that the Kichwa were partly responsible for the Záparas' demise (although Záparas' animosity towards the Achuar was more intense). On several of my visits to the Zápara communities, I heard residents comment that the Kichwa were trying to take Zápara land and had done so in the past.

Moreover, community rejection of DIENAZE teachers seemed to function as a way for Zápara residents to assert local sovereignty by opposing not only the teachers but also Zápara leaders. There often was tension between NAZAE and its constituents because of the substantial geographical distances separating the two. Residents in the Zápara communities did not see their leaders on a regular basis and often imagined them to be "living large" in Puyo. As a Zápara leader once told me, NAZAE constituents saw the organization as being *de oro* (made of gold). Community members assumed that if they were not seeing immediate material benefits from

Figure 4.2 The school in Jandiayacu. Photo by author.

Indigenous organizing, it was because NAZAE leaders were keeping these to themselves.

For community residents, the physical condition of their schools served as the foremost indicator of this imbalance. One afternoon in the community of Jandiayacu, I stood with a Zápara man waiting for a plane to drop government-supplied rice for the community's residents. While we stood in the tall grass next to the hand-cleared runway, he looked at the community's school, located right next to the airstrip, and commented on how it was *muy pobre* (very poor)—a dirt-floored structure with an insufficient number of chairs to accommodate all the students (figure 4.2). In 2003, DIENAZE built a "modern" school in neighboring Mazaramu—with closed walls, a wood floor, and a corrugated metal roof. When I was last there, in 2004, the building was already leaning to one side. Parents grumbled that it had been poorly built and with cheap materials. Issues of funding, equipment, and maintenance of the community schools came up at community meetings and in informal conversations in the Zápara communities. These issues were also the center of discussions among NAZAE leaders and Zápara residents during pan-community reunions like one in July 2004. A woman stood up and demanded to know from Bartolo when repairs were going to be made to the Jandiayacu and Mazaramu schools and when more books and supplies would arrive.

Tension between community residents and NAZAE leaders was also informed by changing attitudes among the Zápara about education—changes resulting from their recent political activism. All the long-term NAZAE dirigentes, like Bartolo, the organization's president for almost eight years, had some formal education in schools outside the communities—an essential component of these individuals' ability to function as leaders within regional and national Indigenous politics. Formal schooling is relatively new in the Zápara communities. Previously, Zápara from the Upper Conambo had to attend one of the missionary boarding schools, such as the one in nearby Moretecocha, or the Indigenous-run school in Sarayacu. Because of the Zápara communities' distance from Ecuador's large population centers, Zápara felt no real pressure to learn Spanish. They did not need it for day-to-day economic or social interactions because Kichwa was (and still is) the dominant language of community life. Most Zápara had no formal schooling, save a few dirigentes whose parents, for one reason or another, had sent them out of the communities to study.

In the process of self-organizing, though, formal education and knowledge of Spanish became tangible indicators of class difference within the Zápara nationality. These represented the basic requirements for leadership in NAZAE and access to the perceived wealth that accompanied such positions. Most Zápara saw dirigentes like Bartolo as living the good life in Puyo—enjoying all the accoutrements of modern life, such as new clothes and shoes, abundant food, and professional work without manual labor. Of course, most Zápara did not see the long hours associated with Indigenous organizing. They saw NAZAE's president only a few times a year and commented behind his back about how much weight he had gained in Puyo. Moreover, instead of the "impoverished" community schools, NAZAE leaders sent their children to schools in Puyo, where they received instruction in Spanish and sometimes limited English, but not Kichwa.

This was not a problem for Zápara parents who saw no reason for their children to learn Spanish. One man in Llanchamacocha told me that he did not want his children to leave the community. Based on his work experiences outside the community, he said that life in Puyo and Quito was difficult compared with life in the rain forest, where his children would have everything they needed. However, during my research, other Zápara began to send their children to attend secondary school in Puyo for at least a few years, if not through graduation. One result of NAZAE's creation was that long-term dirigentes established permanent residences on the outskirts of Puyo, where they planted small plots and built houses similar to those in the communities. Dirigentes and their families represented important resources for people from the communities, giving them a place to stay and an instant social network for navigating the city. Students who left the communities stayed with relatives in Puyo and did not have to come up with money for boarding. Oftentimes, NAZAE was able to create some kind of position or short-term work for students or other community members in Puyo, providing them with a little income.

All of this is not to say that DIENAZE's rural education program failed to institute important aspects of its intercultural agenda. García (2005:87–109) documents similar issues in the implementation of bilingual schooling in rural highland Peru—limited funding, problems with instructors, and tension between activists and parents. However, she argues that, despite problems, rural education programs in Peru created opportunities for residents of rural communities to take a more active role in discussions about their children's future (García 2005:101). As García and others have pointed out (García and Lucero 2004:175; see also Cotacachi 1997), one of the central goals of intercultural education is to empower parents through local participation in community education. DIENAZE's education program created an important space for Zápara residents to put pressure on their leaders—whom they saw as benefiting unequally from Zápara organizing—and to make them listen to the community's demands. One result of this has been heightened tension within the Zápara nationality over differences in leaders' and community members' social mobility. However, there have been positive outgrowths as well, particularly in the area of Zápara language revitalization and education.

Although DIENAZE continues to work on pedagogical materials in Zápara for its instructors to use in their daily lessons, members of the communities are the ones who have become primarily responsible for teaching Zápara language and culture. DIENAZE declared that all Zápara adults were instructors in an attempt to quell community frustrations with hired instructors and involve parents in their children's educations. DIENAZE encouraged Zápara parents to teach important cultural knowledge in the schools. Adults went to the schools once a week to teach skills ranging from building canoes to making pottery. Upon my arrival in these communities, one of the first things many parents did was to take me to the school and show me the results of their recent projects—model canoes, pottery, and student weaving. Parents were often proud and felt empowered by the role they played in bringing the community into the classroom.

At the end-of-the-year ceremony I attended in Jandiayacu in 2004, the only two songs the children performed in Zápara were ones that Carlos, the Zápara-speaking elder, had taught them. Carlos and the other Zápara-speaking elders taught Zápara twice a week in the schools. In the teaching sessions I observed, the elders sat in a circle with the students (many of whom were grandchildren or great grandchildren). The elder would say a word in Zápara and point to something (body parts were a favorite topic). The students then repeated the word until the elder decided that their pronunciation was correct. After a few sessions, the elder would point to something until the students produced the correct word in Zápara, or he would give the students a word in Kichwa and ask them how to say it in Zápara. Because elders did not know how to teach a language in a formal setting, these lessons rarely seemed to progress beyond teaching vocabulary (as opposed to conversational skills).

However, this seemed to be enough for the parents I knew who wanted their children to know some Zápara but did not expect them to become fluent in the language. Learning Zápara was essential for instilling a sense of community identity in their children, but few believed that Zápara would become a routine language in the communities. DIENAZE and NAZAE staff expressed similar understandings of what Zápara language revitalization meant in practical terms—making sure that children were familiar with the rudiments of the language and its symbolic importance for contemporary identity within the nationality. In other words, Zápara language education represents an important subject around which NAZAE and its constituents have unified.

Conclusion

Dialogue between Zápara leaders and community members has been a crucial—if contentious—component of local education. DIENAZE staff have listened to Zápara parents' complaints and taken steps to rectify some of the problems in local schools. In 2006 four Zápara finished their teaching credentials and were employed by DIENAZE in their home communities—an important step that DIENAZE hoped would solve the problem of rapid turnover in instructors. When I visited the DIENAZE office that same year, the new director showed me some of the new curriculum workbooks and a trilingual book of Zápara mythology that his staff had created. The books focused on literacy in Kichwa and, to a greater degree, in Spanish also. These are encouraging steps. Yet, education in the Zápara communities continues to be hindered by broader structural factors. Key among these is the Ecuadorian government's ongoing reluctance to grant Indigenous administrators sufficient funds for quality multilingual education.

In response to this problem, CONAIE has renewed pressure on the government for expanded language rights and funding for Indigenous education. In 2008 the confederation's president, Marlon Santi (an Amazonian

Kichwa activist), campaigned to have Kichwa recognized as an official language in Ecuador's new constitution (drafted by a constituent assembly between November 2007 and July 2008). Monica Chuji, an Indigenous politician and a member of the 2008 Constituent Assembly, argued that adopting Kichwa as an official language would "reinforce its use in the national education system" (*El Comercio* 2008a). Humberto Cholango, the president of ECUARUNARI (Ecuador Runacunapac Riccharimui or Ecuador Indians Awaken), noted similarly that having Kichwa declared an official language would represent "a significant advance in collective rights for [Ecuador's] excluded sectors" (*El Comercio* 2008b).

Recognizing Kichwa—by far the most commonly spoken Indigenous language in Ecuador—as an official national language could serve as a rationale for expanding government funding and education programs for Indigenous languages. If, for example, it were required that government services in Ecuador be provided in Spanish and Kichwa, then the demand for Kichwa translators, bureaucrats, administrators, and instructors would presumably increase. Moreover, the availability of jobs that require knowledge of Kichwa would give students—Indigenous and not—greater incentive to study the language. Of course, this would not augment the use of other Indigenous languages, such as Zápara. This is an issue that other Indigenous leaders have introduced. Although smaller Indigenous languages are official for use in the areas where they are spoken, this does not mean that they are required by provincial governments—something that could reinforce their local use.

Measures similar to these have recently been adopted by Bolivia's government with some (at least short-term) success. President Evo Morales (2006 to the present) has required that all government officials learn an Indigenous language. Enrollment in Quechua and Aymara classes has increased since Morales, who speaks some Aymara, took office in 2006. In 2007 "a student at San Pablo Catholic University…wrote his graduate thesis in Aymara—a first for the country" (*Washington Post* 2007). Bolivia's new constitution, approved in January 2009, gives official status to all thirty-six of the country's Indigenous languages (Bolivia 2009). It requires that national and regional government officials use "at least two official languages, one of which must be Spanish" and "the other will be chosen taking into account the use, convenience, circumstances, necessities, and preferences of the population" (Article 5).

As the Bolivian example suggests, government-mandated support can be an effective means for encouraging the use of Indigenous languages. Thus far, the Ecuadorian government has resisted such support, providing empty recognition for Indigenous languages without real financial or political backing. Since coming to office in 2007, President Rafael Correa has raised government spending for education and supported a clause in Ecuador's 2008 constitution that proclaims the right of all Ecuadorians to universal education through the university level. However, Correa opposed making Kichwa an official language and urged the members of his party—who controlled the majority of seats in the constituent assembly—to vote down proposals to do so (Denvir 2008). As discussed earlier in this chapter, Ecuador's new constitution maintains the primacy of Spanish as *the* official language of Ecuador (Article 2). The document pronounces Kichwa and Shuar to be the official languages of intercultural relations—no one is quite sure what this designation means legally or what its impact will be on Indigenous language education. It is hoped that the vague wording of the new constitution will expand the legal basis for Indigenous leaders to demand that the state more actively promote the use of Kichwa and Shuar (and, later, other Indigenous languages) in official governmental and educational contexts, perhaps along the lines of Bolivia's reforms.

5 External Advocates and the Zápara UNESCO Project

I met Julio on my first trip to Puyo in March 2001. He greeted me with a grin and a handshake outside NAZAE's office, located at the time in an old green building a few blocks from Puyo's main street. Julio asked in thickly accented, but grammatically perfect, English whether I spoke Spanish, and he proposed that we head to Puyo's only pizzeria to discuss the situation of the Zápara language. He hovered over a beer as he told me about the problems of documenting the language: limited budgets for trips to the communities, the difficulty of gathering speakers to record conversations, the trouble many elders had remembering aspects of the language, and so on.

Julio began collaborating with the Zápara shortly after their organization in 1998. He worked with dirigentes to conceptualize, write, and assemble an application to have the Zápara language considered by the United Nations Educational, Scientific and Cultural Organization (UNESCO) as part of its Masterpieces of the Oral and Intangible Heritage of Humanity program. In May 2001 UNESCO granted the request and promised more than $200,000 in funds for the multiyear project. The UNESCO award represented a watershed for NAZAE. Like a springboard, it launched the Zápara to a level of visibility and support they had not previously enjoyed. It also demonstrated the importance of non-Indigenous advocates' assistance in establishing recognition for the Zápara. The application likely would have been impossible without NAZAE's partnership with Julio.

More than a dozen non-Indigenous *solidarios* (advocates) worked in NAZAE during the past decade. Solidarios are not unique to NAZAE (see Rappaport 2005:65–66). In meetings and protests I attended during my fieldwork in the Ecuadorian lowlands and highlands, non-Indigenous Ecuadorians and international activists were present and assisting Indigenous organizations. Yet, as ethnographer Joanne Rappaport (2005:57) notes, the function of non-Indigenous advocates in Indigenous organizations has been generally overlooked in existing literature on Indigenous politics in Latin America, creating a misleading image of internally homogenous Indigenous organizations. Rappaport notes that external advocates have played a significant part in linking local Indigenous struggles to larger movements. This was true of the solidarios active in NAZAE. Most had prior experience in grassroots organizing and came to NAZAE equipped with knowledge of internationally circulating rights narratives—resistance to acculturation, defense of natural resources, and preservation of "traditional" culture. They also possessed higher levels of formal education than Zápara dirigentes, and they were more practiced at writing media statements, drafting grant proposals, and conducting formal studies.

Zápara dirigentes often commented on the importance of the work done by non-Indigenous advocates in NAZAE. However, their reliance on these advocates' skills was a concern. Dirigentes were critical of the role that such skills afforded non-Indigenous sympathizers in shaping the form and content of Zápara projects. This issue surfaced not only during the UNESCO application process but also during the ensuing project. Dirigentes relied on Julio and other non-Indigenous técnicos (experts) to conduct and submit studies that satisfied UNESCO's funding requirements. Furthermore, Zápara dirigentes criticized advocates for not taking the time to mentor Zápara individuals, who hoped to augment their own technical skills through hands-on experience. The Zápara were apprehensive about working with extranjeros ("outsiders" in this context). If they relied too much on solidarios' technical skills in the short term, they would remain dependent on external advocates because they would not be forced to do things on their own (see Rappaport 2005:64).

In this chapter, I examine moments of cooperation and of conflict between dirigentes and their non-Indigenous colleagues during the UNESCO project, in order to provide a nuanced view of the nature of interethnic cooperation in NAZAE. I begin with an examination of UNESCO's restrictive guidelines for recognizing Indigenous expressions of "intangible cultural heritage." I then discuss the role of external advocates in helping NAZAE to fit UNESCO's "tribal slot" (Li 2000:149) and how this process heightened tensions between dirigentes and non-Indigenous advocates. The end result, I show, is that the UNESCO project largely unraveled, failing to deliver much of what the Zápara had hoped the project would do for their organization and language.

"Culture" UNESCO-Style

On May 18, 2001, UNESCO's director general made the first of the Proclamations of Masterpieces of the Oral and Intangible Heritage of Humanity.[1] UNESCO chose the Zápara for the Oral Heritage and Cultural Manifestations award because of their ongoing struggle to "preserve their identity" and their "profound knowledge" of the rain forest (*El Comercio* 2001).

Beginning in the 1970s, UNESCO created a series of recommendations and programs aimed at "safeguarding" global cultural heritage.[2] According to UNESCO's website, the notion of "intangible heritage" emerged in 1997 at the International Consultation on the Preservation of Popular Cultural Spaces convention in Marrakesh. Participants agreed that UNESCO should create an international proclamation to recognize intangible cultural forms, such as "oral traditions" and "traditional craftsmanship" (UNESCO 2003: 1–2). This led to the creation of four major UNESCO programs for intangible cultural heritage: Proclamations of Masterpieces of the Oral and Intangible Heritage of Humanity; Living Human Treasures; Endangered Languages; and the Traditional Music of the World program.

UNESCO privileges Indigenous communities as being essential in the "production, maintenance and re-creation of the [world's] intangible cultural heritage" and emphasizes the importance of Indigenous languages as indicators of cultural diversity (UNESCO 2003:2). The Masterpieces of the Oral and Intangible Heritage program promotes forms of "traditional expression," protects these from cultural standardization, and persuades individual states to safeguard their oral heritages and minority languages (UNESCO 2003:1). In a paternalistic manner, UNESCO constructs "traditional cultures" as museum pieces that must be preserved within the maelstrom of globalization in order for "us" to know what "real" culture is like despite "our" position within a culturally homogenous modernity.[3]

The notion that Indigenous communities merit special attention because of their presumably timeless connection to pre-conquest cultures is not unique to UNESCO but represents the integration of recent transnational narratives of Indigenous rights into the organization's approach to intangible culture. Over the past three decades, a loose network of Indigenous and non-Indigenous activists—what political scientist Virginia Tilley (2002) dubs the "Transnational Indigenous Peoples Movement"—has pursued a set of universal rights for Indigenous peoples (see also Brysk 2000). A significant outgrowth of this "movement" has been the elaboration of a broad package of Indigenous rights in international documents such as the International Labour Organization's (ILO) Convention 169 (1989) and the United Nations' (2007) Declaration on the Rights of Indigenous Peoples (2007), which were drafted in consultation with Indigenous peoples (Tilley 2002:531). This is not to say that these effectively incorporate the entire spectrum of rights demanded by Indigenous activists around the world—many of the most "radical" were excluded in the drafting processes (Nelson 1999:295–301). However, Indigenous activists, national governments, development agencies, and NGOs have looked to both as internationally recognized templates of Indigenous rights. ILO Convention 169 has been ratified by thirteen states in Latin America.[4] Ecuador's 1998 and 2008 constitutions incorporate much of the language of Convention 169 in their statutes on the recognition of Indigenous communities' rights to the use of their languages and ancestral territories. Moreover, the passage of Convention 169 encouraged the World Bank and other development institutions to revise their policies in order to include Indigenous leaders and communities in development planning (Tilley 2005:228).

Both documents stress self-identification as the core component of Indigenous identity and "carefully avoid defining 'Indigenous peoples' beyond general references to 'cultural' distinctiveness" (Tilley 2002:531).[5] For example, ILO Convention 169 frames Indigenous peoples as "tribal peoples...whose social, cultural and economic conditions distinguish them from other sections of the national community" or "peoples" who inhabited a country or region before the "establishment of present state boundaries" and still possess their own cultural institutions (ILO 1989:Article 1). ILO Convention 169 and the UN draft declaration also sketch out rights for which many—but certainly not all—Indigenous activists have campaigned: protection of their languages, access to ancestral territory, and freedom to practice traditional religion (Tilley 2002:531). The UN declaration, for example, emphasizes Indigenous peoples' "distinctive spiritual relationship" to their historically owned or traditionally used lands and resources (UN 2007:Article 25). Both documents also emphasize the importance of preserving and maintaining "traditional" cultural practices, which mark Indigenous peoples' links to pre-Columbian societies and codify their connection to particular locales (ILO 1989:Article 28; UN 2007:Article 13).

The language of Indigenous rights encoded in ILO Convention 169 and the UN declaration has proved useful for many Indigenous organizations because it functions as a guideline for articulating Indigenous demands in a language that resonates with broad, international publics. The problem has been that "outsiders have tended to group these concerns as a package in forming their own model of indigeneity: their understanding of what indigenous peoples *are*, and of what they need" (Tilley 2002:531). Tilley (2005:230) argues that the now "hegemonic model" of Indigenous rights outlined by the ILO and the United Nations does not reflect the realities of many Indigenous peoples, who are not visibly different from non-Indigenous peoples (see also Hodgson 2002:1039). In El Salvador, where Tilley conducted her research, a number of Indigenous people speak Spanish, live in urban spaces, or dress in a manner that is not distinct from "national" culture. During the early part of the twentieth century, Indigenous communities in El Salvador self-identified as Indigenous and spoke Nahua and Lenca (Tilley 2002:531–533). However, following state repression in the 1930s, most began to speak Spanish and abandoned dress that distinguished them from the country's white-mestizos. In the wake of El Salvador's bloody civil war during the 1980s, there was a resurgence of Indigenous identity and pride among communities who had hidden their identities from official view for much of the twentieth century (Tilley 2005:218–222). Recognition and support for these communities, however, were not forthcoming.

Despite the promise of substantial funding for the country's Indigenous communities in UNESCO's Culture of Peace Program, a project aimed at rebuilding post-war national identity, Nahua organizations were unable to secure program support. Nahua concerns were not seen as being "cultural" by UNESCO's standards of Indigeneity (Tilley 2002:550–552; 2005:230). The project sought to fund language revitalization and education programs, but the Nahua wanted credit to buy land, plant corn, and obtain better access to regional agricultural markets. Nahua leaders saw these as a necessary measure for strengthening their collective identity, because corn production "pervades Nahua cosmology, ritual, and worldview" (Tilley 2005:230). UNESCO representatives interpreted the Nahuas' requests as "peasant" issues, because they focused on agricultural development and production, and denied funding for them (Tilley 2005:230). UNESCO representatives wanted Nahuas to focus instead on "Indigenous" issues such as language revitalization and the preservation of folkloric culture.

Anthropologist Tania Murray Li (2000) states that, in order to be acknowledged, Indigenous activists must articulate their demands within the existing parameters of dominant rights discourses (see also Grossberg 1996; C. Taylor 1994). However, activists do have some room to "maneuver as they situate themselves in relation to the images, discourses and agendas that others produce for them" (Li 2000:157). Li stresses that Indigenous activists are able to exhibit agency in the process of selecting which elements of their history and practice they combine to present a coherent identity to outsiders. At the same time, their "room for maneuver may be quite limited" by the fact that "struggles over resources, which are simultaneously struggles over meaning, tend to invoke simplified symbols fashioned through processes of opposition and dialogue, which narrow the gaze to certain well-established signifiers and traits" (Li 2000:157).

In addition to presenting a public image that adheres to dominant stereotypes of Indigenous culture (see Ramos 1998), the process of obtaining recognition from influential international organs like UNESCO requires that activists learn "the relevant legal and bureaucratic categories and processes" (Hodgson 2002:1041). Local activists must file the right forms and paperwork, submit proposals to the right foundations, and document their claims through scientific studies in order to establish recognized links to dominant actors (Hodgson 2002:1041). For many Indigenous groups— particularly the emerging organizations and local communities whose leaders often do not have extensive formal education—this is an overwhelming process that involves navigating the labyrinthine bureaucratic channels of national and international institutions. Many Indigenous organizations like NAZAE have enlisted the help and support of non-Indigenous advocates to aid them in the process of securing external recognition.

Non-Indigenous Advocates

Petitioning for UNESCO support required the Zápara to frame their struggle within internationally recognized idioms of Indigenous culture. They did so by arguing that their rapidly vanishing language represented an enduring link between Zápara collective identity and the rain forest ecology of eastern Ecuador, indicated by their apparent lack of contact with the "outside world." The application process involved formally documenting these connections in a long, multimedia dossier that compiled historical, ethnographic, and linguistic evidence proving that the death of the language would result in the loss of culturally specific information about the Ecuadorian Amazon. At the time, Zápara leaders were not very knowledgeable about how to articulate their cultural identity in a manner that resonated with external publics and donor institutions. They were even less versed in the skills necessary to create and submit the required one-hundred-plus-page UNESCO application. As such, working with Julio was crucial in their bid for UNESCO support.

Julio brought valuable skills to the Zápara project. He was from an upper-middle-class Ecuadorian family and had studied English, French, and linguistics both in Ecuador and abroad. Following his university studies, he collaborated with Indigenous organizations in lowland Ecuador on cultural documentation projects. Julio was uniquely qualified for the UNESCO project, in part because of his ability to write the application in French or English. UNESCO accepts applications only in these two languages, which makes working with an outsider mandatory for most Indigenous organizations in Latin America. Julio also had contacts in UNESCO's Paris headquarters, which helped to ensure the application's full consideration. Moreover, his ability to create—or find other specialists who could create— the necessary sound recordings, photographs, and short video that accompanied the application was vital.

Although Julio was particularly qualified for the UNESCO project, he was not the only solidario active in NAZAE. During my research, other solidarios were working with the Zápara on a host of smaller projects and initiatives; some of them later worked on different aspects of the UNESCO project. Most found the organization through advocacy networks that have increasingly linked Indigenous struggles in the Ecuadorian Amazon to international environmental and human rights campaigns. According to political scientist Pamela Martin (2003:72), the number of NGOs working in the Ecuadorian Amazon increased from almost none in the 1980s to more than two hundred by the late 1990s. As anthropologists Beth Conklin and Laura Graham (1995:696) note, "since the 1980s, indigenous people have become key symbols, as well as participants, in the development of an ideology and organizational networks that link local Amazonian conflicts to international issues and social movements." In particular, Indigenous peoples and non-Indigenous environmentalists "discovered common cause in opposing ecologically destructive dams, roads, mines, and colonization schemes" (Conklin and Graham 1995:695).

Moreover, international environmental groups provided Indigenous leaders with the opportunity to get their message out to a wider audience by circumventing national governments and speaking directly to international audiences (Brysk 2000; Martin 2003). Environmental organizations also validated Indigenous groups' political goals, such as the creation of legal Indigenous territories: "Saving the forest's people was seen as a way to save the rain forest and to preserve its unknown resources that held promise for advances in medicine and pharmaceuticals" (Conklin and Graham 1995:698). However, Conklin and Graham argue that the "greening" of Indigenous politics in the Amazon was not entirely beneficial, because environmentalists' goals did not always accord with those of Indigenous leaders, nor did Indigenous leaders always possess equal footing in discussions about common political projects—issues I discuss in greater detail below. Most of the non-Ecuadorian solidarios working in NAZAE were either employed by or closely associated with an international NGO. Some had come specifically to work with the Zápara. Others had arrived intent on collaborating with one of the larger Indigenous organizations and, dissuaded by these organizations' internal politics, had looked for an alternative.

The largest group of international solidarios active in NAZAE comprised students, volunteers, and professionals supported by a Spanish NGO, Acción

Trans-Atlántica.[6] It supports ethnic resurgence projects, and it gave the Zápara several small grants to improve their organizational infrastructure and paid for several visits by dirigentes to Spain for rights symposia. Some of Acción Trans-Atlántica's volunteers and students worked in NAZAE for only two to three months, often during summer holidays. However, a small group of professional consultants worked with the organization on a more permanent basis, receiving a stipend from the foundation. During my research, three solidarios with education and work experience in fields such as anthropology and biology worked on separate projects aimed at augmenting NAZAE's political and economic independence: a sustainable natural-resource management plan for the nationality, a program for the production and sale of community-made crafts, and technical and legal consulting on mapping the Zápara territory.

All the Spanish solidarios, or técnicos, had previous experience working in broad international solidarity campaigns based in Spain. Two had completed projects with communities in other parts of Latin America and Africa. Acción Trans-Atlántica técnicos focused on specific aspects of the projects they had taken for one- or two-year rotations, but they also worked with Zápara dirigentes to solve general issues that arose in the daily workings of the organization. In many cases, they acted as personal assistants to the dirigentes, helping to coordinate meetings with other organizations, making sure that dirigentes were in the right place at a specified time, and helping to draft interorganizational communiqués and media statements.

Besides the Spanish solidarios, international solidarios most active in NAZAE were anthropology students Anne-Gaël Bilhaut (from France) and I. We began work (independent of each other) with NAZAE for the purpose of conducting studies for our doctorates. Both of us also worked with Zápara dirigentes on NAZAE's cultural projects by helping to write grant applications and reports and conduct short studies for the organization in the Zápara communities. I wrote grant applications in English for language revitalization programs, translated NAZAE applications from Spanish to English so that these could be submitted to international donors, conducted linguistic research with Zápara elders for NAZAE, and wrote a short grammar of Zápara for circulation within NAZAE's education program.

While sharing NAZAE's dedication to Zápara sovereignty, throughout my research I was generally autonomous from the organization. Not only did I have my own motivations (linked to but distinct from NAZAE's political project) for working with the Zápara, but I was also economically independent from the organization. I had funding from graduate student scholarships and grants that I had obtained for the sole purpose of supporting my research project. When in Puyo, I participated in NAZAE's day-to-day operations and helped with whatever tasks Zápara dirigentes asked me to do. Yet, unlike the dirigentes, I came and went when I desired—to Quito for a break and to the United States when school or family obliged. Moreover, as a North American academic, I had economic and social privileges that meant that I did not have to endure the same economic hardships as the dirigentes.

At times, this disparity created tensions between some of the dirigentes and me. At the outset of my research, I met with NAZAE dirigentes to discuss my plans and get their approval for my work. In return for allowing me to conduct an ethnography of the organization, I proposed to collaborate with NAZAE educators and linguists on the documentation of the Zápara language. I presented them with a brief sketch of Zápara grammar that I had compiled from existing sources on the language. All the dirigentes present approved, and Bartolo thanked me for the grammar. It was quickly apparent, however, that I had unintentionally upstaged the director of DIENAZE. He and the assistant director pulled me aside after the other dirigentes had left and strongly repri-manded me. They reminded me that I was a student, not a dirigente, and that it was my job to help them and respect their way of doing things.

I was a bit taken aback by the director's scolding. I had naively assumed that the education dirigente would enthusiastically greet my grammatical work as a helpful boost in documenting Zápara. Having recently completed an MA in linguistic anthropology, I had access to a large research library with grammatical materials on Zápara in Spanish, English, Italian, and French. In contrast, DIENAZE's dirigentes were educated as schoolteachers, had little formal training in linguistic methods, and did not have access to most of the linguistic work done on Zápara. The following day, Oswaldo explained to me that the dirigentes did want my help on the language proj-ect but were apprehensive about working with foreigners. "Someday you will leave," Oswaldo said to me, "and what will happen when we need to teach our own language?" Oswaldo also told me that the process of docu-menting Zápara meant recording more than just *palabras y frases* (words and phrases) as I had done. He said that the language had to be recorded in its entirety, creating a means to preserve broader cultural contexts and mean-ings that were necessary for understanding it. Oswaldo noted that this process might take longer than a standard linguistic analysis but that it was essential to retaining the Záparas' culturally specific perspective on the world. In other words, it was important that I understand and embrace the Záparas' approach to documenting their language. This mutual understand-ing was crucial to fostering equal collaboration between Indigenous and non-Indigenous advocates but was something that foreign solidarios like me often overlooked.

Figure 5.1 Working on a proposal in NAZAE's office. Photo by author.

At times, there were also tensions between me and some of the diri-gentes who were frustrated by what they saw as my inability or unwilling-ness to generate more grant money for NAZAE. Many dirigentes thought that because I was a Northern academic, I had easy access to a plethora of funding sources. Throughout my fieldwork (and afterwards as well), diri-gentes gave me short proposals they had written using a template from the World Bank project (which I discuss in chapter 6) and asked me to trans-late these proposals into English and give them to an American *fundación* (foundation) (figure 5.1). Dirigentes assumed that I had myriad contacts with rich American donors, and they believed that my presence would be enough to guarantee the applications' success. Upon reading many of these grant applications, I told dirigentes that I was not sure where I could sub-mit them. The proposals the dirigentes put together made perfect sense within the specific context of Zápara politics—they either identified con-crete things for which the organization needed money or sketched out the dirigentes' long-term aspirations for their cause. However, the scope of the proposals was either so narrow or so broad that I did not think that they would be evaluated favorably by external donors looking to fund specific projects that fit their particular areas of interest. I offered to work with diri-gentes to identify funding sources or to rework and translate their applica-tions to fit the requirements of foundations with which we were familiar. In most cases, dirigentes insisted that I translate their proposal and send it wherever I could. I did the best I could, contacting friends who I thought might have relevant contacts, submitting proposals to whichever NGOs or foundations I could find. None were funded, and news of a rejection sometimes prompted dirigentes to question whether I had done an adequate job in selling the proposal to potential supporters.

I do not want to give the false impression that my work with NAZAE was riven with tension. Most of my time in NAZAE was characterized by a relatively seamless integration of my research into the organization's operations and my positive relationships with the dirigentes. However, these instances reveal how my work with Zápara activists was informed by differences in our social mobility, material capital, and access to particular bodies of knowledge.

In addition to foreign solidarios like the Acción Trans-Atlántica workers and me, a small cadre of non-Indigenous Ecuadorians worked in the organization, some of whom had long-term connections to Indigenous activism. For example, one of the longest continually employed non-Zápara in NAZAE was the head secretary, a politically progressive mestiza who had worked for another Indigenous organization before taking a job with the Zápara. Most, however, took work in NAZAE more as a stopgap, accepting employment in the organization until something else came along. As the scope and size of the Ecuadorian state shrank during the economic crises of the 1980s and 1990s, the number of employment opportunities in government ministries and universities for Ecuadorians trained in the social sciences and related fields shrank considerably (Uquillas and Larreamendy 2006). Indigenous organizations and NGOs provided important alternatives to government employment for many well-positioned Ecuadorians. For instance, every Thursday a mestizo education specialist left NAZAE's Puyo office and went back to his hometown of Riobamba (roughly five hours away in the highlands), returning for work the following Tuesday morning. Eventually, after several months in NAZAE, he found work in Riobamba as a schoolteacher and never returned. Although working with Indigenous organizations represented a viable option for many non-Indigenous Ecuadorian professionals, many viewed this work as less than desirable.

Julio was no exception to these general trends. He had come to work with the Zápara for a number of reasons: interest in Indigenous languages, empathy for Indigenous politics, and the possibility of working in his field of linguistics. In a conversation we had in 2002, he explained that his wife and he had recently started a couple of businesses in the city where he lived. Because university positions in linguistics are few and far between in Ecuador, and almost always underpaid, Julio explained, the only way he could support his family and still do linguistics work was to combine income from his small business ventures with externally funded language projects. Given his class background, Julio was better positioned in NAZAE than some of the other non-Indigenous solidarios. He had the advantage over international advocates of being Ecuadorian and speaking Ecuadorian Spanish as his first language (a plus with many of the dirigentes, who claimed to have a hard time understanding the Spaniards). Moreover, because of his international connections and education, many of the dirigentes attributed a greater degree of prestige and social capital to him than to the other Ecuadorians working in NAZAE. Yet, as I demonstrate later in this chapter, these qualities also left him open to criticism from dirigentes over his elite status.

Zápara as "Intangible Masterpiece"

Julio worked with Zápara dirigentes to create the Dossier for the Proclamation of the Oral Heritage and the Cultural Manifestations of the Zápara People, the document submitted to UNESCO in spring 2001. In it, the Zápara were portrayed as having struggled to save their way of life as "hunters and gatherers" and to preserve the Zápara language—the only mechanism through which "traditional" knowledge could be passed on to new generations.

Zápara dirigentes co-authored the application with Julio in the broad sense that they were responsible for shaping the scope and content of the project, but they were not active in writing the project proposal. At one meeting I attended in Puyo in March 2001, dirigentes spoke about including the recovery of Zápara shamanic knowledge in the project—something that Julio thought was better suited to a separate project. Zápara dirigentes, however, stressed the importance of shamanism for reviving Zápara identity as a key aspect of reclaiming the nationality's history and as an important emblem of the uniqueness of Zápara identity and cultural practice. Consequently, shamanism was included in the final project application. Zápara leaders also worked with Julio to coordinate and mobilize the community networks that were needed for gathering the initial data for the proposal—trips to the Zápara communities, audio and visual recordings, interviews with the Zápara-speaking elders. Julio drafted, assembled, and translated the final document in relative isolation from the dirigentes. In this capacity, he acted as a kind of conduit, taking dirigentes' ideas, aspirations, and understandings of Zápara identity and rearticulating them in a manner that was presentable and comprehensible to UNESCO project evaluators.

The Zápara application began with a discussion of the Zápara language's function as a vehicle for Zápara cultural memory and how outside economic and social forces threatened its continued use (NAZAE 2001a:5–13). A description of the remaining Zápara speakers followed, with an assurance that all five had a minimal understanding of Spanish and rarely left the rain forest (14–19)—in short, a lack of contact with the modern, nontraditional world ensured the maintenance of their cultural integrity. Later on, the Zápara were described as being "the first inhabitants" (25) of the Ecuadorian Amazon, a region of "the highest biological diversity, natural resources and cultural richness" (64). According to the application, colonization and the incursion of commercial markets, missionaries, and multinational oil companies threatened the "traditional" way of living of the Zápara (65–74). Despite this pressure, the essential core of Zápara culture—the Zápara language—remained intact and unchanged from contact (26). The application argued that the greatest representative of Zápara cultural difference was their language and the knowledge it embodied (26, 30–33).

Julio's audio recording of twelve Zápara songs sung by elder speakers accompanied the written application, along with a short video of "daily" life in the Zápara communities of Ecuador. In the video, members of the Zápara communities were dressed in shirts and skirts made out of fiber from the bark of llanchama trees—clothing that nineteenth-century travel and missionary accounts reported as "customary" Zápara dress (see, for example, Osculati 2000[1848]:144)—to emphasize the "traditional" quality of life in the Zápara communities. These recordings downplayed aspects of Zápara practice in the communities that might have demonstrated "too much" outside influence, bringing into question the pristine nature of Zápara cultural heritage, such as community members' usual clothing of second-hand t-shirts and shorts (see Conklin 1997). In other words, they created an image that more closely fit UNESCO's expectations for authentic Indigeneity than did actual day-to-day life in the Zápara communities. The application ended with a three-year plan for revitalizing the Zápara language, following the guidelines for cultural and linguistic recovery outlined by the 25th General Assembly of UNESCO (NAZAE 2001a:81).[7] Four main objectives were identified: (1) conducting a sociolinguistic census of Zápara in Ecuador and Peru; (2) carrying out meetings between Ecuadorian and Peruvian Zápara to form a binational organization; (3) strengthening education programs in the Zápara language; and (4) documenting cultural practices, especially shamanic ones, associated with the language (91–103).

In an ethnography of rain forest preservation in Indonesia, anthropologist Anna Lowenhaupt Tsing (2005:254) discusses a proposal similar to the Zápara UNESCO dossier, one that was written in 1987 by Indonesian environmentalists working with Indigenous peoples to create a forest reserve. Tsing (2005:254) notes that what was particularly striking about the proposal was that Indigenous peoples, who had organized and fought logging companies, became a "traditional community about to enter history for the first time." Following a common script, Indigenous peoples were portrayed as being "vulnerable and confused"—unable to continue their traditional way of life yet not entirely able to deal with the threats of modernity on their own (Tsing 2005:254). This narrative not only denied Indigenous peoples agency but also reinforced the need of non-Indigenous "experts"— "civilized people who reach out to touch the wild [and] can speak for it at the edge of its destruction"—to intervene in behalf of Indigenous people and direct their actions (Tsing 2005:253).

In the same vein, the Zápara dossier afforded little agency to the Zápara and much to external advocates. The Zápara were determined to preserve their language, but the application made this seem impossible without the intervention of UNESCO-approved "experts" like Julio. These experts would bring "modern" techniques in linguistics, ethnography, and education to the Zápara in order to ensure that their language was properly documented, the boundaries of their culture group were officially delineated, and their community education was sufficiently improved.

Tsing (2005:254) argues that the role of the "expert" is twofold: "to record, advocate, and revere, on the one hand, and to guide, manage, and modify, on the other." Put another way, experts would preserve Zápara culture but would also give it a "tuneup" to make sure that it continued to run in the twenty-first century despite its decidedly pre-modern hardware. Tsing (2005:254–255) warns against examining too closely the contradictory representations of Indigenous culture in proposals like the UNESCO application, because these reflect obvious efforts to conform to external expectations. But she notes that these contradictions are "important in examining cultural gaps and linkages" (Tsing 2005:254). The contradictions contained within the Záparas' proposal are illustrative not only of the limitations of UNESCO's model of Indigenous culture but also of the tensions these created between Indigenous dirigentes and non-Indigenous advocates working on the documentation project. Indeed, tensions between dirigentes and advocates played a central role in undermining the UNESCO project.

Cooperation and Conflict

Although UNESCO approved the Zápara application in May 2001, funding for NAZAE's project did not begin until 2004. During this period, NAZAE leaders met with personnel from UNESCO's Quito office and were told that financing for the project was being sought but had not yet been secured. Throughout much of my time working in NAZAE, Zápara dirigentes hoped that the money they had banked on to jump-start their language revitaliza-tion program would come in another month or two. After completing a small documentation project, Julio left NAZAE in search of other projects. When I returned to Puyo in summer 2002, I met him at a restaurant near the center of town. He explained that he could not continue to work with NAZAE because there was no funding—a great disappointment after the work he had done to get the UNESCO project approved. He sighed with exasperation, saying that the UNESCO funding was probably locked up in international bureaucracy and he did not know when (if ever) it would come through. In the meantime, he tried to initiate a similar project with another nationality and secure government funding for it.

In addition to a dearth of funding, Zápara dirigentes cited personality conflicts as a reason for Julio's departure. María claimed that Julio had not adjusted well to working in the communities. According to her, Julio never wanted to make long trips into the communities because he did not want to be away from his home and businesses and did not like living in the rain forest. As a result, he subjected the elderly Zápara speakers to overly long linguistic elicitation sessions (in María's opinion) so that he could collect the data necessary for his project in short trips. Furthermore, Oswaldo main-tained that Julio was short-tempered and impatient with the dirigentes. Julio often talked down to the dirigentes, making them feel as though they did not understand what needed to be done to obtain external support for the revitalization of Zápara or that they took too long to make decisions about how to move forward with the project.

Nonetheless, Julio was back working in NAZAE on the first phase of the UNESCO project when funding materialized in 2004. The Japanese govern-ment's permanent delegation to UNESCO earmarked $203,956 for the Zápara from its Funds-in-Trust for the Preservation and Promotion of the Intangible Cultural Heritage, and another $70,000 was provided by the Sheikh Zayed Bin Sultan al Nahyan Prize.

Julio's return was indicative of the level of interdependence between the dirigentes and him. Participation in the project provided Julio with supple-mentary income and an opportunity to work as a linguist (his preferred profession), as well as to see a project on which he had already spent con-siderable time come to fruition. Regardless of personality tensions, the Zápara needed individuals like Julio to conduct the "expert" work—popu-lation census, linguistic analysis, and so forth—for which they themselves were not trained. In order to elicit the kind of "concrete" and "scientific" documentation of Zápara language and culture that UNESCO required, each of the project's core components was led by an outside "professional" or "expert." According to one dirigente, these professionals were vital because they could develop methods for ensuring that the Zápara would learn their own language in a quick and easy fashion. An Ecuadorian specialist in bilingual education oversaw Phase I of the Zápara project (the linguistic census), helping to structure the census document that would be used, analyzing the final data, and drafting a report to UNESCO on the status of the language. The actual field operations for this phase were led by Julio and one of the ATA workers who traveled to communities in Ecuador to administer the census.

During Phase I, María was appointed as an assistant to the field census team. She acted as a guide and translator for them; neither Julio nor the Spanish volunteer spoke Kichwa. When I asked María about her role as an assistant, she said that she did not like having to work again with Julio, whom she found overbearing. However, she commented that working as an assistant was ideal for her because she did not want to deal with the technical side of the linguistic survey and was able to focus on talking to the Zápara-speaking elders. She told me that she had always been more interested in history and that traveling along the Conambo and Curaray rivers gave her a better sense of the Záparas' historic territory. Not all of the dirigentes were equally content with the project's structure, however. Some who were working to obtain technical training and degrees felt that they were forced into a subordinate role in the UNESCO documentation project.

Oswaldo, who was studying linguistic documentation and Indigenous education at Universidad de las Nacionalidades Indígenas de la Amazonía Ecuatoriana (UNIDAE), was dissatisfied with dirigentes' level of involvement in the project. He said that he understood the need for non-Indigenous experts because there was immediacy to the project—documenting the number of speakers and the language to make sure that it was "done right." He reasoned that the dirigentes did not have enough time to learn how to do a complete linguistic documentation of Zápara because of the age of the speakers and the relatively limited time frame of the UNESCO project. However, Oswaldo expected that the project would provide more of an educational opportunity for the dirigentes than it did. He had hoped to sharpen his linguistic skills and understanding of writing formal grant reports for use on future projects by collaborating with Julio and the other non-Indigenous técnicos. Yet, Zápara dirigentes were mostly responsible for managing project logistics—working out transportation issues, supplying food, arranging meetings in the communities, and translating.

Non-Indigenous "experts" generally left Puyo and the NAZAE office to assemble the data they had collected and write up their project reports at home in Guayaquil and Quito. This was understandable, given that—as I mentioned for Julio—the UNESCO project was not the only source of income or the only project in which some of these non-Indigenous técnicos were involved. They had courses to teach, businesses to run, and families to attend to. Oswaldo acknowledged this but also emphasized that it was vital for dirigentes to be involved in this aspect of the project, to get inside the process of producing final reports and technical documents. If nothing else, non-Indigenous técnicos' ability to compile their results elsewhere emphasized the differences in class and social mobility, as well as the uneven dependence between the two groups. If the project did not work or if a técnico no longer wanted to continue, he or she could leave. In comparison, dirigentes either were more attached to the project because of its importance to the future of the nationality or had fewer opportunities for other kinds of professional employment.

To illustrate this, Oswaldo mentioned that one of the UNESCO project specialists refused to make her data available to the Zápara. Nor did she write a final report of her activities, which UNESCO required from NAZAE. Oswaldo claimed that the disagreement was over how much input and involvement the dirigentes had in the portion of the project for which this specialist was responsible. However, one of the Acción Trans-Atlántica workers with whom I spoke maintained that the issue was dirigentes' mismanagement of project funds—individual leaders used the money to fund their own personal projects or treated it as personal income. In the meantime, the Zápara had to contact another specialist to redo the necessary work quickly and submit a project report. This instance reveals the Záparas' dependence on non-Indigenous advocates and the power that advocates potentially derived from this inequity.

Shaky Alliances

This final point was perhaps best illustrated by a Canadian solidario who was active in the early planning stages of the UNESCO project. Lloyd was a middle-aged North American who acted as a broker between NAZAE and external supporters and worked closely with Zápara dirigentes to formulate future projects. He was not active in writing the UNESCO application or working on the project. However, he obtained small grants from North American foundations to fund some of Julio's initial linguistic work on the Zápara language and finance the production of audio and visual recordings of the Zápara speakers.

Lloyd had a short temper and a penchant for waxing romantic about the nobility of Zápara cultural connections to the Ecuadorian rain forest. During the late 1990s, he came into contact with NAZAE through North American and Ecuadorian solidarity networks. Lloyd was involved in NAZAE's daily operations on a more sporadic basis than the Spanish solidarios, visiting Ecuador a few times a year for stays ranging from a few weeks to a couple of months. Nonetheless, he was involved in shaping the image of the Zápara that NAZAE projected to international audiences. He co-authored web articles and emails for solidarity mailing lists. He was also economically dependent on the Zápara—much of his annual income came from a fee that he charged for the grants and donations he obtained in their name.

A few months after UNESCO recognized the Zápara, I received several emails from Julio asking me to help resolve a conflict that had erupted between Zápara dirigentes and Lloyd. According to Julio (and several dirigentes to whom I spoke the following year), Lloyd had been skimming more than his prearranged 10 percent fee from the money he collected for the Zápara. When several dirigentes accused him of soliciting donations in their name and stealing the money, he reportedly left Puyo in huff. Without Lloyd, the Zápara had no way of accessing the money he had raised for them. They emailed me to ask whether I could contact a foundation that had apparently given several thousand dollars to Lloyd for Zápara language documentation. I was unsuccessful in contacting the donor, about whom the dirigentes had no information save a foundation name. The foundation did not have a web page and was not listed in any of the phone directories I checked, nor was its name familiar to any of the individuals active in solidarity work whom I asked. What I gathered from earlier conversations with Lloyd was that the "foundation" was a tax shelter for a rich retiree fascinated with "exotic" Amazonian Indians; it consisted of little more than someone writing checks from time to time.

Lloyd solidified his position as a necessary intermediate by keeping the Zápara in the dark about the specifics of this grant. Lloyd's normal practice was to ask contributors to give their donations directly to him and to deposit them in his personal bank account. When he arrived in Ecuador, he would make a withdrawal from his account for what he considered the proper amount, minus his fee, and give that to the Zápara. In this case, the Zápara had a record only of how much money Lloyd had given them, leaving no way to ascertain whether he had helped himself to more than his allotted fee. Whether or not he took more than his fair share, what is evident is that Lloyd dealt with the Zápara in an opaque manner, ensuring their dependence on him as a go-between with North American donors.

This raised the ire of several dirigentes who had expressed their frustration with Lloyd during my first visit to Puyo in 2001. They thought that he had too much say in Zápara matters and wanted him to leave. They complained that Lloyd had more power than many of the dirigentes because he was able to buy influence with the money, clothes, and equipment he brought on each of his visits to Puyo. Lloyd did little of the day-to-day work necessary in the organization and had few technical skills the organization needed. But when he visited the Zápara communities, he expected the families to host and feed him. After the dirigentes' blowout with Lloyd, he left Puyo and did not contact the Zápara for several years. Not everyone, though, was glad he left. On a number of occasions, Bartolo lamented that although Lloyd had done an unfortunate thing, Bartolo felt that he had learned a great deal from his North American colleague and missed his support. Bartolo told me that he hoped other North Americans would choose to work with NAZAE, because the organization benefited from working with international solidarios.

Many volunteers working in the Ecuadorian Amazon are held accountable to their Indigenous collaborators. The best NGOs are clear and upfront about their organization's goals, their reasons for working with Indigenous peoples, their operating procedures and policies, and the sources and amounts of their funding. This does not mean that policies of accountability and transparency are the cure-all for conflicts between non-Indigenous and Indigenous activists, as many development agencies would have it. The tensions between non-Indigenous solidarios and Zápara activists that I detail in this chapter are not reducible to issues of accountability, but are fueled by broader societal inequalities in education and social mobility. Nonetheless, as Lloyd's example demonstrates, accountability and transparency are essential prerequisites for initiating and sustaining a productive collaboration between foreign solidarios and Indigenous activists—a foundation for addressing deeper issues of dependency and inequality in such collaborations.

Conclusion

Interaction between Indigenous leaders and non-Indigenous solidarios has been crucial in obtaining external support for NAZAE's local struggle. In this regard, cooperation in NAZAE resembles the situation described by Rappaport (2005:57–58, 62), who demonstrates that Indigenous organizing in southern Colombia has emerged from a "deep and sustained dialogue between native activists and non-Indigenous allies" engaged in an intercultural exchange at the "heart of the Indigenous movement." Non-Indigenous activists have occupied an instrumental position within Colombia's Indigenous organizations, providing not only "technical capabilities that… Indigenous leaders lacked" in the early stages of organizing but also introducing "critical perspective[s]" on citizenship to Indigenous rights debates (Rappaport 2005:57, 63). Yet, it would be far from accurate to describe cross-cultural collaboration in NAZAE as a model of interethnic cooperation, as

Rappaport does. Relationships between dirigentes and non-Indigenous advocates were cooperative but were also characterized by feelings of frustration and conflict and relationships of dependence.

Rather than see unity among participants as a requirement for collaboration, Tsing (2005:246) urges us to view collaboration as having "friction at its heart." As she puts it, collaboration is not consensus but an "opening for productive confusion" (Tsing 2005:247). In support of this assertion, Tsing discusses the creation of a community-managed forest in Indonesia that was made possible by collaboration among Indigenous villagers, "nature lovers," and urban nationals. Although these advocates were united by a common cause, "the varied, and equally satisfied, protagonists never came to a shared agreement about what happened" (Tsing 2005:246). Despite this, all the participants were equally content with the final result—sparing the forest from corporate destruction. Tsing (2005:245, 247) uses this example to argue that "differences invigorate social mobilizations"—the more dissimilar advocates are, the more they have to struggle to create "barely overlapping understandings of the same situation." In the process, they make "wide-ranging links" possible, creating the possibility for "new objects and agents" of change to emerge (Tsing 2005:247).

In Tsing's focus on the positive qualities of friction within collaboration, her analysis tends to overlook the negative effect that this same friction can generate within movements and organizations. As anthropologist Orin Starn (1999:187) observes, "Unity in protest is never completely possible, because diversity of opinion and concern can be a resource as well as a liability." He notes that internal cleavages (especially around gender) in the peasant justice movement he examined in Peru undermined the movement's goal of furthering social equality. This is perhaps the most appropriate frame for understanding collaboration between Zápara dirigentes and non-Indigenous solidarios in NAZAE—a series of relationships that eludes any simple explanation. The initial stage of the UNESCO project stood as an example of cooperation among dirigentes and their non-Indigenous advocates. However, there were also moments of conflict and distrust that were related to broader inequalities within Ecuadorian society. UNESCO's project framework exacerbated such cleavages with its emphasis on the primacy of outside "experts" in documenting Indigenous knowledge. In short, it put a project that promised to augment local Indigenous autonomy firmly in the hands of non-Indigenous directors, reinforcing notions of the supremacy of elite knowledge and relationships of local Indigenous dependency on outside support. In the end, friction within the project apparatus resulted in something with which none of the participants was wholly satisfied.

6 The World Bank, Ethno-development, and Indigenous Participation

On a cloudy day in October 2002, I sat in NAZAE's office conversing with one of the Zápara dirigentes about Ecuadorian politics (figure 6.1). It had rained earlier in the day, leaving the afternoon cooler than usual. I asked Oswaldo what he thought of the upcoming presidential elections; the final vote was less than a month away. He leaned back in his chair and said that he thought the candidates were not all that different—the important thing was that the next president sign a new agreement with the World Bank. I was puzzled by this statement and pointed out that behind his desk was a three-by-five-foot poster decrying the actions of the World Bank and the IMF. I told him that I had thought that Indigenous people were opposed to the World Bank. Oswaldo wiped his forehead with the back of his hand before sitting up in his chair and patiently explaining Indigenous peoples' stance on multinational financial institutions. He said that CONAIE and CONFENIAE had opposed the restrictions the World Bank had placed on loans to Ecuador because they would have forced Ecuador to privatize Indigenous land. Oswaldo explained that, in addition to opposing such restrictions, Indigenous organizations pressured the World Bank to provide funding for local Indigenous development initiatives aimed at augmenting Indigenous autonomy. In his estimation, this funding now made up a significant portion of the budget of most lowland Indigenous organizations (this was certainly true for NAZAE). Oswaldo thought that if the incoming president did not make an agreement with the World Bank to continue these

Figure 6.1 Zápara dirigentes discussing organizational strategies at their office in Puyo. Photo by author.

funds, there would be another Indigenous uprising like the one that had taken place the preceding year.[1]

Oswaldo referred to a World Bank–funded development initiative known as the Proyecto para el Desarrollo de los Pueblos Indígenas y Negros del Ecuador (Ecuador's Indigenous and Afro-Ecuadorian Peoples' Development Project, or PRODEPINE). In 1997 the World Bank approved a $25 million loan for PRODEPINE—an "ethno-development" initiative to fund grassroots development and education programs to address the "strong correlation between being indigenous and being poor" (Van Nieuwkoop and Uquillas 2000:5). The World Bank lauded PRODEPINE as its first project "to focus exclusively on indigenous peoples" (Van Nieuwkoop and Uquillas 2000:4). This was also the first time Ecuador borrowed money specifically for the benefit of its Indigenous population and the first time Indigenous organizations collaborated with the government on development (Van Nieuwkoop and Uquillas 2000:4). It was accompanied by the creation of the Consejo de Desarrollo de las Nacionalidades y Pueblos del Ecuador (Development Council of the Nationalities and Peoples of Ecuador, or CODENPE), a new Indigenous-run government ministry.

The World Bank claimed that PRODEPINE was a bottom-up project created to address the particular economic hurdles that individual Indigenous communities faced. The main thrust of the project was to work with local Indigenous organizations to design and implement "demand-driven" development projects that addressed specific community needs. In addition to funding such projects, PRODEPINE sought to "empower" local actors by conducting in-house training for the staff of Indigenous organizations, partnering small organizations with local NGOs, and expanding the physical infrastructure of Indigenous organizations (PRODEPINE 2002:3). However, I demonstrate in this chapter that PRODEPINE did not empower NAZAE leaders to implement their own development initiatives. PRODEPINE's staff enforced strict parameters on the kinds of projects it chose to fund, ones that stressed economic decentralization more than Indigenous political autonomy (Van den Berg 2003). The project fostered a paternalistic relationship between PRODEPINE and NAZAE, encouraging the Záparas' dependence on external funding and failing to give them the tools to attain economic sustainability.

Social Capital

PRODEPINE was part of the Bank's broader effort to mitigate the impacts of (as well as popular opposition to) structural adjustment programs by focusing on the social aspects of economic development, or what Bank analysts refer to as "social capital." Between 1998 and 2001, the Bank created the Social Capital Initiative, a series of international studies funded to explore the usefulness of social capital in creating economic adjustment programs "with a human face" (Bretón 2005:37). Political scientist Victor Bretón (2005:33–40) argues that Bank experts have employed the notion of social capital as a way of combating criticism that its policies are strictly monetarist and do not consider the social effects of structural adjustment. Moreover, by highlighting social capital in new development programs, Bretón (2005:35) argues, Bank experts could appear to incorporate up-to-date social theory into their approaches without having to accept the aspects of those theories that may be critical of neoliberalism (see also Li 2007:231).

Similarly, economist Ben Fine (2001, 2003) deplores the lack of critical acumen in the World Bank's use of the term *social capital*. The concept of social capital is most closely associated with social theorist Pierre Bourdieu (1977, 1986), who defined it as the resources that accompany an individual's position within existing social hierarchies and networks of unequal exchange. Fine (2003:590) notes that liberal economists and development specialists have modified the term, stripping it of Bourdieu's structuralism and taking it to stand loosely for all non-economic social interactions.[2] Fine (2003:587, 598) rightly argues that this "fungible" notion of social capital ignores the specifics of historically rooted economic relationships, replacing them with the blanket notion that all poverty is reducible to questions of social capital. Put another way, people are poor not because of structural limitations and historical marginalization, but because of their own lack of know-how or because of their cultural deficiencies.

As Fine (2003:591) points out, Bank staffers emphasize the importance of grassroots participation in creating social capital. However, they stress that it can be activated only from outside (Bretón 2005:45), thus rationalizing the need for experts to intercede in behalf of local communities, providing the "remedial intervention" that communities require to correct the "pathology of traditional ways" and ensuring that local projects adhere to Bank precepts (Li 2007:232, 250; Shepherd 2004; see also Rose 1999). In this vein, PRODEPINE and other ethno-development projects have been premised on the idea that development experts, by providing necessary external input, can empower "non-modern" people to make successful and sustainable forays into the "modern" economy (Lind 2005:59).

Indigenous Development

In the case of PRODEPINE, the World Bank (1995b) decided that giving Indigenous peoples better access to finance and education was the best means for "activating" their social capital and thus alleviating poverty (Radcliffe 2001:140). Despite possessing "high level[s] of social capital" (Uquillas and Larreamendy 2006:27), Indigenous people in Latin America consistently experienced higher rates of poverty than non-Indigenous peoples (PRODEPINE 2002:1; Psacharopolous and Patrinos 1994). World Bank analysts reasoned that this was because preexisting forms of traditional social capital were not analogous to those necessary in "modern administrative/economic and even social infrastructure management" (Uquillas and Larreamendy 2006:27).

In keeping with this prescription, the majority of PRODEPINE's funding was allocated for micro credit, education vouchers for Indigenous people, and training for local organizations (PRODEPINE 2002:16–23). Project staff and affiliated NGOs provided technical advice and training for local organizations to learn to identify development problems, create plans for solving them, solicit funds, and execute successful projects. This training was intended to "strengthen" Indigenous organizations' "human capital and local social capital" (PRODEPINE 2002:5). PRODEPINE (2002:6) also sponsored programs to "rescue" Indigenous peoples' "material patrimony and cultural inheritance"—paying for the publication of ethnographic and historical works and Indigenous language dictionaries and for festivals that showcased Indigenous difference. Bank experts emphasized language as a dual indicator of an individual's membership in an "ethnic" community and of exclusion from "mainstream" Ecuadorian society (Van Nieuwkoop and Uquillas 2000:16). These same analysts noted that "households in which an [I]ndigenous language is spoken are more likely to be poor than are Spanish-speaking households" (Van Nieuwkoop and Uquillas 2000:6). PRODEPINE (2002:6) financed linguistic documentation as a way to help mitigate the "cost" of being identified as Indigenous within Ecuador's labor market, by strengthening local cultural pride and enhancing non-Indigenous peoples' "tolerance and respect" for Indigenous culture.

This attention to local cultural difference seemingly departed from earlier top-down development programs that sought to erase "backward" aspects of local practice that elite institutions viewed as "impediments" to modernization (Elyachar 2002:500; Lind 2005:59–60; see also Escobar 1995). Development paradigms from the 1960s and 1970s stressed state-centered national economic programs. However, since the 1980s the World Bank has emphasized the need for bottom-up programs that take into account the cultural particularities of specific communities and local actors (Li 2007:230, 238). Bank experts' rationale for this approach was that local Indigenous communities were better equipped than state agencies to evaluate local economic problems.

The World Bank's 1999 Country Assistance Evaluation Report for Ecuador stressed that prior lending to the country relied too heavily on the executive branch of the national government (World Bank 1999:3). According to the report, Ecuador's central government was unreliable, corrupt, and not fully committed to reforms, which were also thwarted by opposition from the national legislature and "major interest groups" (World Bank 1999:2–3, 11). To reduce future risks to Bank investment, the report proposed a reduction in money to the state and a more sustainable "participatory approach" to development that would focus on working directly with local actors (World Bank 1999:3). Bank experts theorized that local Indigenous communities possessed "natural capacities for self-management" that were "damaged" by top-down development projects (Li 2007:230). Empowering communities, the World Bank hoped to unleash "hidden entrepreneurial qualities of the Third World poor" to define their own projects and transform the economy from the ground up (Elyachar 2002:496).

Yet, far from responding to local voices, the Bank's social development programs have refashioned local micro practice to more closely fit its macrolevel economic adjustment initiatives (Li 2007:231). Analyst Maarten Van den Berg (2003) argues that World Bank staffers were willing to employ a limited range of solutions for addressing "ethnic" poverty in Ecuador— those that were consistent with the Bank's macroeconomic reform policies. Like other World Bank "community-driven projects," PRODEPINE was not designed to produce an "equal outcome" among its participants, but the necessary conditions for equitable participation (Li 2007:242).

As evidence of this, Van den Berg (2003) notes that World Bank staffers ignored structural aspects of Indigenous poverty when designing PRODEPINE. For example, the call for a "more equitable distribution of land has been (and still is) a rallying point of ethnic activism" in Ecuador (Van den Berg 2003:5). But according to Van den Berg, World Bank staff adamantly opposed funding for significant land reform as part of PRODEPINE because it would not improve Indigenous communities' access to off-farm wage labor (see World Bank 1997:5). He notes that Bank staff argued that its resources were best spent on improving Indigenous peoples' situation in the labor market—despite declining opportunities for formal wage labor in Ecuador (see Bourguignon, Ferreira, and Lustig 2004). In the end, PRODEPINE authorized a paltry $405,355 for land purchases in order to resolve existing conflicts over property already occupied by Indigenous families (PRODEPINE 2002:30–31).

Re-forming CODENPE

PRODEPINE identified Indigenous communities and their local organizations as the obvious agents for carrying out ethno-development programs. Local Indigenous organizations were lauded by the World Bank for their strong sense of "belonging to a community," attachment to "communal territory," unique systems of self-government, "solidarity through collective works, and joint celebrations and communal calendars" (Van Nieuwkoop and Uquillas 2000:6). Despite this emphasis on the primacy of local associations, political scientist José Antonio Lucero (2003) argues that PRODEPINE created an opportunity—albeit unintentionally—for Indigenous activists at the national level to institutionalize the notion of plurinationalism within the Ecuadorian state. CONAIE's leaders accomplished this through the restructuring of the Ecuadorian counterpart to the World Bank's project, CODENPE—a process detailed by Lucero (2003:32–40), whose analysis is summarized in the following paragraphs.

CONAIE's leaders argued that they were excluded during the initial stages of PRODEPINE's planning and pressured the interim government of President Fabian Alarcón (1997–1998) to create an Indigenous development agency that would take part in any Indigenous development initiatives in Ecuador. In response, Alarcón created the Consejo Nacional de Planificación de los Pueblos Indígenas y Negros del Ecuador (National Planning Council for the Indigenous and Afro-Ecuadorian Peoples of Ecuador, or CONPLADEIN) to work with the World Bank in planning PRODEPINE. The problem for CONAIE was that each of Ecuador's national Indigenous federations received a seat on the council's governing board. The confederation's leaders did not think that they should have the same voting power as organizations that no longer claimed a substantial base of representation (Lucero 2003:36; Van Cott 2005:109). The confederation responded to this situation by pressuring newly elected president Jamil Mahuad (1998–2000) to get rid of CONPLADEIN and replace it with CODENPE—a change that Mahuad made by presidential decree. In contrast to CONPLADEIN, CODENPE was "organized not by national confederations, but by 'nationality' and, in the case of the largest nationality, the Kichwa, by the smaller unit of pueblo" (Lucero 2003:36).

Lucero (2003:32) argues that this move consolidated CONAIE's "hegemony...in setting the terms for indigenous representation" in Ecuador. However, he points out that implementing a council of nationalities was no easy task, given that Ecuador's Indigenous groups were not officially organized as such (Lucero 2003:38–39). PRODEPINE staff intended to work exclusively with what it designated as "second-tier" organizations—regional organizations that acted as links between grassroots organizations and national umbrella federations (Van Nieuwkoop and Uquillas 2000:6). Second-tier organizations were assumed to have a more direct relationship to the individuals and communities they represented, were in a "better position to know local needs and demands," and garnered credibility from national Indigenous organizations because of their close links with base populations (Van Nieuwkoop and Uquillas 2000:12). Coordinating with second-tier organizations was meant to give PRODEPINE a "more deeply rooted and more solid base of support for the project, and reduced the risk of facing politically motivated decisions by a few Indigenous leaders at the top" (Van Nieuwkoop and Uquillas 2000:12).

However, PRODEPINE staff faced the problem that there was a dearth of well-equipped second-tier organizations in the Ecuadorian Coast and Amazon, which have lower population densities and fewer organizations than the Sierra (Lucero 2003:39). This absence of second-tier organizations, combined with pressure from CODENPE, resulted in PRODEPINE's concession to work with nationalities "where there was no other option" (Lucero 2003:39). Given the situation, PRODEPINE staff incorporated a component in the project for strengthening the organizational and administrative capabilities of small nationalities so that they could function as second-tier

Figure 6.2 A police officer standing across the street from the entrance to CODENPE's office in Quito; the national capitol is visible in the background. Photo by author.

organizations. PRODEPINE's willingness to work with these nationalities not only represented a victory for CONAIE but also provided a political opening for the Zápara.

Ethno-development and the Zápara

On April 30, 2003, I stepped out of the 10 de Agosto trolley with several Zápara leaders and trudged up one of the steep hills in Quito's historic district, where we made our way towards CODENPE's office, an old stone building tucked down a side street near the capitol (figure 6.2). The Záparas' mission that day was to get one of CODENPE's directors to sign a document that would declare their organization the representational body of the Zápara nationality in Ecuador. We had been to the office the day before, after a jolting night bus ride got us into Quito just as the sun was rising. The official who needed to sign the document, the *secretario ejecutivo* (executive secretary), was not in, so we were forced to stay the night and wait another day. When we arrived at CODENPE the next morning, a receptionist informed us that the secretario ejecutivo was in, and we were led quickly to a cramped office on the second floor. After some small talk, the document was signed, copies were made, and the secretario ejecutivo was off to another appointment.

The document officially made ONZAE (Organization of the Zápara Nationality of Ecuador) into NAZAE (Zápara Nationality of Ecuador). The shift was a subtle one and did not mark an internal transformation in the organization. In practice, ONZAE had functioned as the Zápara nationality's representative in CODENPE since 1999. Inclusion in CODENPE's governing body meant that the small, newly formed organization had—in theory —equal footing with much larger, better organized nationalities such as the Shuar or the Amazonian Kichwa. On a pragmatic level, it helped the Zápara to gain important support from other Indigenous leaders and organizations. Drawing on this support, the Zápara asked for CODENPE's recognition as a nationality in 2003 in order to settle their ongoing battle with the Comuna Záparo over official representation of the nationality. CODENPE's recognition laid this dispute to rest (at least momentarily). CODENPE's decree proclaimed that the organization had been responsible for the "reconstitution, unity and fortification of the [Zápara] nationality." Conversely, it declared that the leaders of the Comuna Záparo had not worked towards the development and unification of the Zápara nationality and that NAZAE represented the majority of Zápara in Ecuador.

Although the Záparas' participation in CODENPE has been an important long-term source of political legitimacy and inclusion within national Indigenous politics, NAZAE's participation in PRODEPINE yielded only short-term gains for the nationality. The Zápara fit into the project's goal of strengthening the administrative capacity of small Indigenous nationalities. A PRODEPINE survey claimed that there were speakers of the Zápara language still living in Pastaza province and that approximately six hundred individuals (an exaggerated number) self-identified as Zápara in seven communities (PRODEPINE 2002:19). PRODEPINE funded three main initiatives for building and strengthening the Zápara nationality: reinforcing a sense of Zápara cultural pride and identity, improving the physical infrastructure of NAZAE's office, and training NAZAE's leaders in project development and grant writing.

As a step towards developing local Zápara sovereignty, PRODEPINE encouraged the recovery of Zápara-specific cultural practice and the validation of local Zápara knowledge (PRODEPINE 2002:7). One of the first things PRODEPINE did was to fund a radio communication program, installing shortwave radio stations in Llanchamacocha, Jandiayacu, and the NAZAE office in Puyo with the intention of increasing communication between the organization and its constituents. PRODEPINE also provided money for the publication of Zápara pedagogical materials for distribution within the communities, including a series of children's coloring books with brief literacy exercises in Zápara. Apart from educational materials,

PRODEPINE sponsored the publication of a short Zápara dictionary (Andrade 2001) and a history of the Zápara in Ecuador (Trujillo 2001).

These measures were aimed at building a "sense of community" among the geographically dispersed Zápara settlements by highlighting the "positive qualities" of their shared "culture" (Van Nieuwkoop and Uquillas 2000:1, 5). A working document that PRODEPINE provided to the Zápara stated that it was crucial to identify, preserve, and cultivate the "best" aspects of local cultural practice and experience because these were vital for generating positive interactions and trust among community members. In turn, the interactions and trust—which the document labeled as a group's *energía cultural* (cultural energy)—represented the most important source of motivation for communities to "face their problems, look for solutions, and participate in putting them into practice" (PRODEPINE n.d.). As a first step towards harnessing their cultural energy for collective good, the document encouraged local organizations to initiate a "community self-diagnosis," which involved identifying positive aspects of a community's cultural patrimony, as well as negative ones that needed to be "enriched" through individual or collective "intervention" (PRODEPINE n.d.; see also Van Nieuwkoop and Uquillas 2000:19).

Despite this emphasis on community-directed self-analysis, PRODEPINE staff retained significant control over the course that local development initiatives took (see Li 2007:249). The training materials PRODEPINE provided to NAZAE stressed that before local communities or organizations initiated any self-diagnoses or interventions, they should first consult with PRODEPINE staff to define the objectives of the exercises, identify the participants, and discuss possible incentives for participation (Van Nieuwkoop and Uquillas 2000:17–18). The reason for such oversight was that PRODEPINE staff assumed that small organizations like NAZAE did not function systematically when analyzing community problems—something that development planners saw as a clear shortcoming in local Indigenous communities' social capital. As an immediate solution to this perceived shortcoming, PRODEPINE staff closely oversaw Zápara subprojects. In the long term, they hoped to solve this by improving NAZAE's administrative capacity: establishing a permanent office space for the organization in Puyo, purchasing office furniture and machines, and providing training and supervision for NAZAE's staff.

What emerges here is a clear paradox: PRODEPINE celebrated Indigenous peoples' "social capital" but reasoned that local actors could not put it to responsible use without external supervision and funds. Unsurprisingly, rather than become more autonomous, NAZAE became dependent on PRODEPINE funds—a serious problem when the project ended and

NAZAE was left with half of its previous operating budget.[3] I returned to Ecuador in 2004, after a six-month writing and working sojourn in the United States. During this period, NAZAE moved its office from the spacious, centrally located second floor of Puyo's new Bell South building to a cramped, mildewy apartment several blocks from the town center. The size of the organization's administration also shrank—several familiar faces were no longer present in the office because funding for their positions had evaporated. NAZAE was enabled to stay afloat when funding for the first phase of UNESCO's language documentation project emerged that year. However, the money was limited, compared with PRODEPINE's prior funding, and was allotted for a narrower range of activities and personnel. When UNESCO funding stopped in 2007, NAZAE moved yet again to a more decrepit and smaller office.

Oswaldo, who had been active in the Záparas' education program since its inception, was one casualty of the organization's downsizing. In 2006 I ran into Oswaldo's wife on my way to NAZAE's new location. She said that he was not working there anymore and that if I wanted to see him, I should visit their house just outside Puyo. After greeting people at the NAZAE office, I waited at the front until one of Oswaldo's younger sons came by. We walked together along Puyo's cobbled streets, which eventually gave way to the unpaved, muddied roads of the poor, semi-rural area where Oswaldo had a wooden house and a small garden plot. Oswaldo was happy to see me and welcomed me inside. He had grown out his hair and his beard—something that seemed out of place to me because I had always seen him well-dressed and looking like a consummate professional in the NAZAE office. He explained to me that he rarely left his house anymore because of the debts he had amassed. He had been out of work for almost a year at that point. Initially, he was employed on a short-term contract through MEC to develop a new Zápara curriculum. However, the contract was for only two years of work and could not be extended. After that, he was employed in the first phase of the UNESCO project, but when that ended, there was no funding for his position. NAZAE did not have any projects running that could employ him, because it had not been successful at obtaining any new grants.

Talking to Oswaldo made me wonder why NAZAE had been unable to find more funding. After all, PRODEPINE's promise was that it was going to make small organizations and nationalities like the Zápara self-sufficient—they would write proposals and get grants for development programs and small business ventures and not have to rely on state money or big development projects to sustain themselves. PRODEPINE was presented as a grassroots, bottom-up development program. Yet, it replicated the clientelism of earlier development schemes: bureaucrats at the top awarded funding to authorized local organizations that adhered to PRODEPINE's guidelines for implementing subprojects (Bretón 2005:73).

During my 2006 visit, I also talked to Jorge—who was employed by an NGO called Cooperativa Amazónica (Amazonian Cooperative)—about problems with PRODEPINE's approach to small nationalities.[4] According to Jorge, PRODEPINE's solution to NAZAE's "problems" was to inject a large sum of money into the organization over a short period of time with the idea that if NAZAE's size and budget expanded, PRODEPINE could fast-track the organization to self-sustainability. PRODEPINE more than doubled NAZAE's budget in the span of a few years, most of the money going to organizational strengthening—a quite flexible category that covered a broad range of expenses from office equipment to travel to work stipends. According to Jorge, this encouraged young and relatively inexperienced Zápara leaders to view development projects as sources of income, which they used to improve the organization's financial situation and their own individual finances. Zápara leaders waited until the money ran out, and only then did they look for other sources of revenue. As a consequence, Jorge said, the Zápara never really "got" the concept of projects. By this he meant that Zápara leaders had become quite savvy at getting public recognition for their organization but had not learned to "work the development system." They were ineffective at repackaging their organization's goals into finite development projects that addressed specific community needs and attracted external funders. Jorge thought that the process of writing applications and applying for grants employed a culturally specific Euro-American logic with which Zápara leaders were unfamiliar.

One of PRODEPINE's promises, however, was to remedy this situation, expanding Záparas' opportunities for improved training and education by doing two things. First, PRODEPINE funded twenty-two scholarships for Zápara youth to complete their high school degrees, plus five more for students to complete college-level training. These scholarships had little to no effect on Zápara educational attainment—only one individual completed his degree program (PRODEPINE 2002:24). In 2004 I talked to Zápara who received scholarships but had been unable to complete their degrees because they lacked sufficient financial resources for travel and boarding.

Second, PRODEPINE required NAZAE leaders to collaborate with NGOs that could provide regular institutional support, consultation, and mentoring (Van Nieuwkoop and Uquillas 2000:17). Cooperativa Amazónica partnered with NAZAE to develop a comprehensive development plan for the nationality and identify long-term projects and goals. Furthermore, the Spanish volunteers discussed in chapter 5 worked with

NAZAE leaders to help them execute the short- and long-term plans they had set out for their organization. More than school vouchers, PRODEPINE staff saw this kind of collaboration as the most important source of training for burgeoning organizations like NAZAE because it was hands-on and specific to the organizational challenges the nationality faced (PRODEPINE 2002:7).

One of NAZAE's primary goals was to solidify title to the Zápara territory. As I mention in chapter 2, NAZAE's communities are located in two government land blocks with separate titles. In order to better unify the nationality, Zápara leaders wanted to consolidate their legal land base and create a national territory. In 2003 I sat in on a number of meetings among Zápara leaders, Cooperativa Amazónica staff, and government officials on the subject of the Zápara land title. The first took place in Puyo on April 15 and included Jorge, Bartolo, and two other Zápara dirigentes, as well as Julia, a Spanish advocate from Acción Trans-Atlántica. Jorge began with a presentation of ideas or strategies that the Zápara could use for developing a pragmatic plan of action for legalizing their territory—what fees needed to be paid to what government agencies, what needed to be done to map the territory, and the like. For the most part, the Zápara participants were quiet. They did not offer much in the way of support or criticism of Jorge's presentation. Julia asked questions and pitched suggestions. In general, Jorge and Julia dominated the conversation, with Bartolo and his colleagues offering little commentary. At one point, towards the end of Jorge's presentation, Bartolo spoke up, saying that he was concerned that the people in the Zápara communities did not have enough involvement in the territory project, which would not work if they did not understand its importance for the nationality. Julia interjected, saying that this could be solved by having one of the leaders travel to the communities to explain the project in Kichwa. Although Bartolo commented that it might be difficult to explain ideas like "organizing" and "collective land rights" to Zápara individuals who were not familiar with these concepts, in the end he deferred to Julia's suggestion. After the meeting, Julia wrote up a plan, which she later circulated to Jorge and the NAZAE leaders.

Afterwards, the other two Zápara present, who had said almost nothing, played with dominant gender associations and joked that, because of Julia's assertiveness, she was really a Zápara man, not a Spanish woman—an indication that at least some of the dirigentes were not comfortable with the level of control Julia and Jorge had exerted in the meeting. As I explain at the end of chapter 5, this was a recurring point of tension between dirigentes and external advocates. Instances like the one above struck me as odd —I was dismayed at how such meetings often sidelined Zápara dirigentes while reinforcing the authority of outsiders. However, a meeting I attended on April 29 in Cooperativa Amazónica's office underscored some of the problems that Zápara leaders had in navigating official legal and administrative processes.

At the meeting, four Zápara leaders presented Cooperativa Amazónica with a proposal to map and acquire title to their territory. They claimed that the process would cost $10,000 and asked Cooperativa Amazónica for a $6,000 loan towards the project. During the meeting, Jorge raised several issues with the Záparas' proposal. First, he explained that the title would need to be registered with the Instituto Nacional de Desarollo Agrario (National Institute of Agrarian Development, or INDA) in its Ambato office, not in Puyo, as the Zápara had said in their proposal. Second, to ensure that the project would be completed, he wanted to know who was going to provide the other $4,000.

The Zápara explained that their lawyer—an unreliable figure from Ibarra who left the organization shortly afterwards—had told them that they only needed to register the title in Puyo. As to the question of where the rest of the money would come from, Bartolo explained that CONFENIAE promised to guarantee Cooperativa Amazónica's loan. When Jorge noted that CONFENIAE had not given the Zápara anything in writing, Bartolo said that UNESCO would probably give them money for mapping their territory. Jorge pointed out that UNESCO's funding for the project had not yet come through (it would not for another year, it turned out) and questioned whether it included funding for the Zápara territory—a query that Bartolo was unable to answer.

After making several phone calls to engineering firms, Jorge told the Zápara that mapping their territory should cost only $4,000. He said that they needed to get an official quote from an engineering firm to confirm the price. Moreover, they needed to get legal copies of the existing land titles and written agreements from the communities stating that they would consent to merging their old titles into one. In the end, Jorge explained to the Zápara that it is always important to talk to several lawyers to make sure that they have a clear and accurate picture of the legal procedures they need to follow, as well as to get written documentation from the parties involved.

For both Jorge and Julia, with whom I spoke afterwards, this meeting presented a revealing example of NAZAE's difficulty navigating unfamiliar legal processes. While both grumbled about problems and inadequacies within the "system," they also acknowledged that other avenues of financing simply did not exist for Indigenous organizations. Moreover, they noted that NAZAE's lack of knowledge about these official channels reinforced the need for external advisors like themselves to consult with NAZAE and ensure that it was not duped and received what was rightfully due.

PRODEPINE's assumption that collaboration with outside NGOs would foster learning and improve the organization's institutional autonomy was faulty at best. What this instance suggests is that it reinforced the Záparas' dependence on NGO support. On April 24, 2003, I attended a meeting in NAZAE's office during which several dirigentes voiced their frustration with the PRODEPINE project. Diego, DIENAZE's director at the time, spoke about the importance of preserving Indigenous ways of doing things and notions of development. "We cannot just learn from outsiders," he said, "We need to have more of a cultural exchange so that learning goes both ways." He went on to say that if the purpose of development was to make Ecuador more democratic, then development agencies should recognize different ways of doing things, different kinds of knowledge, not just the kind that outsiders have. "Right now there is no real development, just talk of development," he said.

Conclusion

On a warm afternoon in late 2002, I asked Mauricio, who was from Llanchamacocha, about PRODEPINE and what it had done for the Zápara communities. "That project did nothing for us," he replied. "We still do not have any way of making money to buy clothes, or machetes, or plane flights." PRODEPINE primarily funded projects that were meant to increase intracommunal relationships that could serve as the basis for developing market-appropriate social capital, such as the radio program and the publication of books on the Zápara. The effect that these materials had on community solidarity was dubious at best.

PRODEPINE had an almost unnoticeable effect in the communities, but it had a pronounced impact on NAZAE. PRODEPINE's decision to work with small nationalities meant that the Zápara, who would have been bypassed by the original project proposal because of their size and administrative weakness, were included to help strengthen their organizational capacity. Although NAZAE was likely more influenced by participation in the project than were older organizations with more experience working the parameters of external development programs, NAZAE's experience with PRODEPINE was similar to that of other Indigenous communities and organizations.

In a study of the project in the Ecuadorian Andes, Bretón (2005:67) argues that it would be hard to underestimate the negative effect that PRODEPINE had on Indigenous activism. According to Bretón (2005:42, 52), PRODEPINE was one of the largest development initiatives in Ecuador's history, giving the project tremendous influence over local discourses of activism and ethnicity. The project significantly reshaped the spaces of recognition open to Indigenous organizations in the Ecuadorian Andes, limiting the action of the region's Indigenous organizations by encouraging a shift from protest to *proyectismo* (project-ism) (Bretón 2005:69; see also Ferguson 1990; Mallon 2005:183). In a conversation in May 2003, Oswaldo summarized this point nicely: "Indigenous people know how to organize themselves, to make demands and stage uprisings, but now we are expected to create projects and write proposals to get anything done."

PRODEPINE's insistence on working with local organizations led to a "boom" in the number of small nationalities and pueblos in Ecuador because communities found that they needed second-tier organizations to get resources (Bretón 2005:52–55). In a background paper for the World Bank, Lucero (2006b:24) notes that PRODEPINE focused on second-tier organizations because these represented the "densest layer of associational life capable of carrying out development programs." However, using social capital to guide PRODEPINE's policy meant that the areas receiving the most help were often "not the ones with the greatest needs, but rather with the greatest [organizational] abilities" (Lucero 2006b:24–25).[5] Certain areas—such as the southern Sierra province of Loja, which has not been as attractive to development organizations because it is too isolated or not Indigenous enough—obtained fewer resources than provinces such as Chimborazo, which is considered one of the most Indigenous provinces in the Ecuadorian Andes (Bretón 2005:61). Bretón (2005:23) argues that this led to escalating tensions among communities and organizations, as well as an increased fracturing of the Indigenous movement at the national level.[6] Moreover, the project reproduced the status quo by ignoring structural inequalities and attributing Indigenous poverty to a lack of local initiative— or, in Bank terms, the ineffective use of social capital.

Epilogue
Looking Back, Moving Forward

I returned to Ecuador in 2006 after being gone for more than a year and a half. I had spent the spring and summer of 2005 finishing graduate school in California and then moved halfway across the country to start a teaching position in Iowa. Only days after my summer course on globalization ended, I boarded a plane in Des Moines, headed for Houston and then Quito. My flight was delayed and I missed my connection, which forced me to spend a day waiting in Houston for the next plane. When I finally arrived in Quito, the sun was rising, casting orange-pink light on the newly remodeled Mariscal Sucre airport (another airport is currently under construction just outside Quito). After a short wait in the customs and immigration line, I was greeted by a sleepy official who stamped my passport, and in no time I was outside the building and in a taxi. I asked the driver, a middle-aged man with salt-and-pepper hair, to take me to a small hostel near downtown Quito. The two of us chatted for most of the fifteen-minute ride. We made some small talk about Ecuador's prospects for advancing in the soccer World Cup, and then I asked him what he thought about the state of the country's economy. In his estimation, more tourists were flying into Quito, which meant more cab fares for him. Before dropping me off at the hostel, he said that things were never really good in Ecuador but were a little better than they had been a few years before.

After checking in to the hostel and having a quick rest, I drank coffee with one of the owners, whom I had befriended during my many stays in Quito. Business at the European-style pensione had been good, and he showed me the renovations and additions he had made since my last visit.

Later that afternoon, I talked with an Ecuadorian friend who had recently graduated from university. A few months before, he had married a Canadian woman who was working for a nonprofit organization in Quito. I asked whether they were going to move to Canada and was surprised when he said that they planned to stay in Ecuador, because the overwhelming number of Ecuadorians I knew who had married foreigners had left in search of better economic prospects. My friend explained that his partner and he liked living in Quito and did not want to leave. Moreover, he said, the economy had improved, so they did not feel the necessity to leave. According to him, prices had finally stabilized, six years after the country's adoption of the US dollar as its currency. His partner and he made enough money to rent an apartment near one of the city's central parks, eat in restaurants, and pay for health care.

The next day, I left the hostel early, took a taxi to the bus station, and caught the first bus to Baños, where I switched to another headed for Puyo. When I first traveled to Puyo, in 2001, it often took several hours from Baños along the winding road that served as one of the main transportation links between the Ecuadorian highlands and eastern lowlands. Parts of the road were dirt, and some sections narrowed to a single lane with a cliff face on one side and a sheer drop on the other. When traffic was heavy, buses would meet head-on and engage in a slow dance of backing up and inching forward to make it around each other, stopping traffic in both directions. While I was gone, the government had improved the road—double-lane tunnels now bypassed the more treacherous spans, and new pavement covered much of the way. Consequently, I got to Puyo earlier than expected and had enough time to drop off my bag at a hotel before visiting the NAZAE office.

The organization had moved offices while I was gone. Before my visit, one of the dirigentes had emailed the street address for the new office. However, the street names in Puyo are not well marked, if at all, and I had a difficult time finding the small side street where the new office was located. After walking in a few circles around the same block and stopping to ask for directions twice, I luckily ran into Zápara friends. We walked a couple of blocks together and then stopped in front of a small white house near Puyo's center. There was no sign on the outside to indicate that it was NAZAE headquarters, but as I approached the front door, I noticed the metal sign that once hung outside the Záparas' old office propped up against a wall. Only a few people were inside the office, which was otherwise empty (figure E.1). After saying hello to everyone, I went to the corner store, brought back some cookies and soda, and then sat down to catch up with those who were present. Over the course of the next two weeks, I made

Figure E.1 Inside the NAZAE office, 2006. Photo by author.

daily visits to the office and walked to the outskirts of town to see Zápara friends who no longer worked for the organization.

I was struck by the changes NAZAE had undergone in the time I was away. In contrast to the indicators of economic prosperity I had heard about and seen on my way to Puyo, NAZAE was a shadow of what it had been just a few years before, when it occupied the entire floor of one of Puyo's largest downtown office buildings. Between 2001 and 2004, the Zápara office had often buzzed with the activity of a dozen or more dirigentes, their spouses, and their children. It seemed almost vacant during my return trip. As the previous chapters attest, the preceding years had not been without their problems for NAZAE—intragroup conflicts, issues with external advocates, difficulties retaining economic support. I had realized at the time that these would continue to cause trouble for NAZAE. Yet, because the organization possessed considerable forward momentum and what seemed like a durable network of support, I had assumed that it would overcome any roadblocks and continue to function. Combined with troubling developments in Ecuador's national politics, however, these issues had put NAZAE into a tailspin.

Increased Restrictions

Six months after I left Ecuador in 2004, I received an email from María. "Estamos mal, Max [We're in a bad way, Max]," read the first line. NAZAE was suffering politically. Its problems were linked to Lucio Gutiérrez's election to Ecuador's presidency in 2003. Nowhere were the restrictions of officially endorsed multiculturalism more apparent than in the Gutiérrez government's dealings with Indigenous leaders. The former army colonel campaigned in green fatigues and styled himself as the next Hugo Chavez, promising sweeping economic and social reforms. Once in office, he donned a suit and met with IMF officials to discuss Ecuador's future, insisting on the need for economic austerity and entrusting the country's finances to "well-known bankers with neoliberal tendencies" (Almeida Vinueza 2005:100). According to Ecuadorian analyst José Almeida Vinueza (2005:100), "although Gutiérrez also ceded the Ministries of Agriculture and Foreign Relations to two prominent [I]ndigenous leaders, he disrupted their administration by subjecting them to the guidelines of the regime, which...was completely associated with the International Monetary Fund and the US Embassy." Former CONAIE president and Gutiérrez's minister of agriculture Luis Macas said that Gutiérrez "didn't even take into account the plan to strengthen national agriculture in Ecuador that [the Ministry of Agriculture] had elaborated" (Geertsen 2006).

In response, ECUARUNARI quickly "withdrew its support for the government and demanded the resignation of the ministers responsible" for accepting austerity measures that Gutiérrez proposed in an agreement with the IMF (Zamosc 2004:148). However, CONAIE did not publicly denounce the president for another three months and delegates from its political party, Pachakutik, continued to work in the government until its ministers were expelled by Gutiérrez in August 2003. Following Pachakutik's ouster, "the internal divisions of the [Indigenous] movement rose to the surface"— leaders from the Sierra criticized CONAIE for not leaving the government sooner, but organizations in the northern Amazon castigated the confederation for not staying in the government and working things out (Zamosc 2004:149). Gutiérrez capitalized on this discord and worked to undermine "the Indigenous movement by fomenting internal divisions among its principal organizations" (Almeida Vinueza 2005:100; see *El Comercio* 2004b).

In 2005 Nelson Chimbo, the Gutiérrez-appointed secretary of CODENPE, gave NAZAE's seat on CODENPE's governing board to the Comuna Záparo. This decision came at a difficult time for NAZAE, because it no longer had PRODEPINE funding and was struggling to stay afloat economically. María and her brothers had been working to consolidate a legal title for the Zápara territory but abandoned their efforts and turned to regaining NAZAE's seat in CODENPE. Tensions between the Zápara organizations escalated to the point that María and other NAZAE dirigentes feared for their own safety. A year later, two Zápara dirigentes were ambushed and beaten in what appears to have been a politically motivated attack.

Similar tensions reverberated through other Indigenous organizations in Pastaza province. OPIP and CONFENIAE split into pro-CONAIE and pro-government factions, threatening the survival of both organizations (El Comercio 2004a). Gutiérrez appointed Antonio Vargas—a lowland Kichwa leader and former president of CONAIE who participated in the 2001 presidential coup—as head of the Ministerio Bienestar Social (Ministry of Social Welfare). Vargas worked to marginalize lowland activists loyal to CONAIE, accusing them of corruption and of channeling money away from anti-Gutiérrez organizations in the Oriente.[1]

Gutiérrez's heavy-handed style of governance soon caught up with him, and he was ousted by popular protest in April 2005. The national legislature unanimously voted to eject Gutiérrez from office and replace him with the vice president, Alfredo Palacio. Protestors surrounded the national capitol—forcing Gutiérrez to retreat by helicopter and flee to the Brazilian embassy. Weakened by two years of internal and external battles (Zamosc 2004:152), CONAIE played only a minor role in the protests (Burbano de Lara 2005).

Since CONAIE's founding (and indeed throughout much of Ecuador's history), Indigenous peoples' power has lain in "their capacity to disrupt and in their ability to sustain this disruption over time" (Pallares 2002:224). As sociologist Leon Zamosc (2004:152) notes, CONAIE and Pachakutik collaborated with the Gutiérrez government in the hope of consolidating a position for themselves within the Ecuadorian state, effectively moving from a "politics of influence" to a "politics of power" in which they would be able to "leave the mobilizations behind and achieve objectives by participating in the decisions of the state." Zamosc (2004:152) argues that the problem was that Indigenous participation in the state remained dependent on the president's "authority to define the composition of the cabinet and its modus operandi," enabling Indigenous leaders to exercise only "fragments of power."

Following Gutiérrez' ouster, CONAIE focused on reuniting its base and rebuilding alliances with social organizations such as unions and student groups. In 2006 Luis Macas was re-elected as CONAIE's president (he had led the organization from 1990 to 1996). Shortly afterward, Macas led a March 2006 mobilization that shut down the country for several days. In contrast to CONAIE's failed 2004 uprising, the confederation's sometime rival Federación Indígenas Evangélicos del Ecuador (FEINE) participated, as did CONFENIAE. CONAIE demanded that interim president Alfredo Palacio (2005–2007) withdraw from free trade talks with the United States, cancel its contract with Occidental Oil (a Los Angeles–based company), and convene a constitutional assembly to declare Ecuador a plurinational state (*Washington Post* 2006).

Palacio reacted by declaring a state of emergency, suspending constitutional law, banning public meetings, and imposing a curfew (*Washington Post* 2006). Despite Palacio's negative reaction to the demonstrations, he later announced that Occidental Oil's contract would be turned over to PetroEcuador, the state-run oil company. On May 16, the Bush administration broke from free trade talks with Palacio's government, citing Ecuador's actions against Occidental as an indication that the country was not willing to play by the rules of international free trade (*Boston Globe* 2006).

The cancellation of Occidental's contract and the end of Ecuador–US trade talks were important victories for CONAIE as it reestablished the confederation's "combative credentials" (Zamosc 2004:150). Following these wins, CONAIE put renewed pressure on the Ecuadorian government to declare the country a plurinational state. ECUARUNARI's president, Humberto Cholango, claimed that the recognition of Ecuador as a plurinational state was a vital step towards decolonizing the Ecuadorian government (Lucas 2008).[2] According to Cholango, multiculturalism reinforced "neoliberalism and the folklorization of Indigenous peoples" (Becker 2008b). In contrast, he argued, the concept of plurinationalism advocated a complete reorganization of the Ecuadorian state and would lead to a more just distribution of political and economic resources (Becker 2008b).

In November 2007, Ecuador convened a constituent assembly to rewrite the nation's constitution. The assembly's draft constitution was made public the following July. The text of the new constitution recognized Ecuador's plurinational character. Yet CONAIE and its member organizations did not immediately endorse the proposed constitution (*El Comercio* 2008c, 2008d, 2008e). The process of drafting the constitution was largely co-opted by President Rafael Correa (2007 to the present), and the document lacked many of the substantive changes that CONAIE leaders wanted, such as prior consent for resource extraction on Indigenous territory (Becker 2008c; Denvir 2008). However, opposing the constitution would have allied Indigenous leaders with the Ecuadorian right, which opposed Correa's state-centric economic and social reforms (Becker 2008c; ECUARUNARI 2008). In the end, Indigenous leaders could not pass on the opportunity to have plurinationalism protected in their country's primary governing document, so they backed the new constitution, which was approved by national referendum in September 2008 (Denvir 2008).

Picking Up the Pieces

In May 2008, I was in Ecuador for a week to work on a grant proposal with a colleague and conduct research in one of Quito's archives. I was unable to travel to Puyo and meet with NAZAE leaders. However, since my last visit to NAZAE in 2006, I have kept up with developments in the organization through phone calls and emails with Zápara friends. Following Gutiérrez's ouster, CODENPE reinstated NAZAE as its representative of the Zápara nationality. A few months later, a cousin of one of the Comuna Záparo leaders formed a new organization called the Nacionalidad Sápara de Ecuador (Zápara Nationality of Ecuador, NASAPE). Apparently, in 2006 he convinced CODENPE to give NASAPE a seat on CODENPE's governing board. The following year, CODENPE returned the seat to NAZAE with pressure from CONFENIAE and CONAIE. Sadly, the dispute between the two organizations continues as each petitions different government officials and Indigenous politicians to support its side.

All of this occurred at a time when NAZAE was undergoing a change in leadership. Since its founding in the late 1990s, NAZAE had had only one president: Bartolo Ushigua. Bartolo was a charismatic leader who developed savvy public relations skills and cultivated important national and international connections during his seven-year tenure as the organization's president. In 2005 he left Ecuador, taking important political experience with him. Consequently, at a time when seasoned leadership was most needed, the organization was left in the hands of Bartolo's less experienced (and timid) brother. In 2007 the organization moved its office yet again, this time to a small building on the outskirts of Puyo. The rent was paid using money from the organization's small, state-allocated budget for administering education in the Zápara communities. Bilingual education is the one operation that NAZAE has been able to pursue with some consistency over the past three years. DIENAZE still receives annual government funding, which has given it a reliable economic base to continue its projects. In contrast, NAZAE's political operations were on hold from late 2007 to mid-2008 for lack of funding.

In summer 2008, María organized elections for new dirigentes in the hope that NAZAE could be resuscitated. Although the new leaders chosen by the Zápara communities are young men, María and one of her younger sisters have come to occupy a central role in the organization. As the oldest dirigente active in NAZAE, María possesses important political knowledge and a network of contacts that younger leaders lack. She now holds a solid position of authority in the organization, given her age and institutional memory. Moreover, she has been mentoring her sister, who grew up spending considerable time in the NAZAE office. María's sister has become involved in coordinating NAZAE's operations and its interaction with other organizations and supporters. This development seems to indicate that new space for Zápara women activists and leaders has emerged in the organization.

The young dirigentes who now direct NAZAE are the age—early to mid-twenties—that Bartolo and many of the former Zápara dirigentes were when they began the organization a decade ago. This shift in NAZAE's leadership could be invigorating for the organization. These leaders represent the first generation of Zápara to come of age immersed in Indigenous politics and activism—some of them literally grew up in the NAZAE office, playing and doing homework while their parents and relatives discussed the future of the organization. Moreover, some of these dirigentes have gone to school or hung out with youth from other Indigenous nationalities, forging alliances that may help the small Zápara nationality to weather future crises. Anthropologists Kay Warren and Jean Jackson (2005:567) note that the future of Indigenous activism centers on questions such as these: Will youth continue to forge ahead with plans to establish official territories? Will they find other struggles or modes of activism—working for an NGO, for example—more appealing for personal, political, or financial reasons? Or will they abandon activism?

For now, these young activists seem to be intent on reestablishing their communities' organization. At the time of writing, NAZAE dirigentes are working to organize a pan-community reunion to discuss a new Plan de Vida Zápara (Zápara Livelihood Plan), which would outline the important issues confronting the nationality and propose creative ways to solve them. They are also collaborating with the residents of Llanchamacocha to build a new school outside the community. The structure will serve as a meeting place for the reunion and be used in the future as a center for community-based training sessions on various aspects of community organizing and activism. The building will also house a new biology classroom, where students from the communities can study environmental threats to their territory and the importance of mapping Zápara lands. These projects appear to signal a return to building solidarity within the nationality. Moreover, they indicate efforts to work around traditional state and NGO funding in order to forward Zápara goals—the community center is being built with volunteered labor and donated materials. Projects like this may help NAZAE to become less dependent on external inputs, thus fortifying the nationality's autonomy.

Recently, I received an email with a PowerPoint presentation that several of these dirigentes had put together to show their long-term plans for a unified Zápara territory—an indication of their improving literacy and technological skills. Several Zápara are now pursuing high school and advanced training degrees in Puyo. This may enable them to deal with external solidarios on a more equal footing and to take a more active role in designing and writing project proposals for their organization. However, NAZAE dirigentes continue to struggle with securing enough funding to maintain an office in Puyo. As I demonstrate in chapters 5 and 6, the ability to apply for and obtain external funding is not dependent solely on access to formal education. It also involves specific knowledge about how to articulate grant projects in a language that is recognized by external donors. This is not being taught to Zápara leaders in formal education programs.

To address this issue, Zápara dirigentes have expressed a desire for more international volunteers with expertise in development and conservation to help them with components of their short- and long-term plans for the Zápara nationality; one asked whether I could put interested students in contact with the organization. However, despite Zápara activists' desire to attract new volunteers, at the time of writing I know of no full-time solidarios in the organization. Long-term advocates like the European solidarios who were active in NAZAE (and me) continue to provide support "from afar," translating grant applications and looking for potential sources of funding for the Zápara. However, the Zápara do not have the same in-house support that they did in the past, when solidarios not only helped to flesh out grant applications but also coordinated meetings with potential donors. Though making it more difficult for NAZAE to tap in to external funding, the absence of solidarios in the organization may be beneficial, giving Zápara activists greater control over the direction of their organization and, as noted above, encouraging them to find alternatives to the established funding system.

As these recent updates demonstrate, the Záparas' story denies any neat conclusion. NAZAE continues to struggle for meaningful change for itself and the communities. Despite the Záparas' persistence and dedication, NAZAE's future prospects are still unclear as the organization continues on a shoestring budget. Yet, NAZAE's story plainly illustrates the limitations imposed on local Indigenous activists by official discourses of multiculturalism in Ecuador.

Political scientist Donna Lee Van Cott (2006) argues that, in countries with relatively weak Indigenous movements, strong neoliberal elites have been able to limit the adoption of radical Indigenous rights. In contrast, Van Cott (2006:285) points to Ecuador as an example of powerful Indigenous resistance overcoming relatively weak elite opposition to gain "a foothold in the formal political system for the articulation of more radical, transformative alternatives." Van Cott's analysis is based on a brief survey of the number and character of Ecuador's reforms in comparison with those of other Latin American states. Indeed, many of Ecuador's legally enacted multicultural policies are "more expansive" than those that are on the books in other countries (Van Cott 2006:295). However, the reality is that their implementation has been uneven. Moreover, the expanding role of the private sector in economic development has meant that Indigenous com-munities are increasingly subject not only to the requirements of the state but to those of non-state organizations as well (Hale 2002:489). Although many preach local Indigenous empowerment, the Záparas' participation in UNESCO and World Bank projects demonstrates how both undercut NAZAE's ability to further its own political agenda, by increasing its dependency on outside help and money. In short, multicultural reforms have not provided the Zápara with an effective foothold for bringing about changes in their situation. Granted, NAZAE's size and inexperience put it at a disadvantage when navigating the complex processes that are now necessary for securing external support. But, as noted above, Gutiérrez's multiculturalism wracked Ecuador's most powerful Indigenous confederations.

This book highlights the challenges that multicultural reforms have produced for the Zápara, thus offering a window into the difficulties faced by local activists in their attempts to redefine Ecuadorian politics. As such, this book underscores the need for ongoing ethnographic studies of large-scale reforms. In addition to Ecuador's current "post-neoliberal" government, Bolivia and Venezuela have proposed and enacted broad programs of "new socialism" aimed at more equally distributing wealth among their citizens. In the coming decade, on-the-ground studies of these antipoverty reforms will be important for understanding whether this shift has provided new openings for local Indigenous activists to move beyond the restrictions of multiculturalism.

Acronyms

AIEPRA	Asociación de Indígenas Evangélicos de Pastaza Región Amazónica (Association of Evangelical Indians of Pastaza in the Amazonian Region)
ANAZPPA	Asociación de las Nacionalidad Zápara de la Provincia de Pastaza (Association of the Zápara Nationality of Pastaza Province, which later became NAZAE)
CODENPE	Consejo de Desarrollo de las Nacionalidades y Pueblos del Ecuador (Development Council for the Nationalities and Peoples of Ecuador)
CONAIE	Confederación de Nacionalidades Indígenas del Ecuador (Confederation of Indigenous Nationalities of Ecuador)
CONFENIAE	Confederación de Nacionalidades Indígenas de la Amazonía Ecuatoriana (Confederation of Indigenous Nationalities of the Ecuadorian Amazon)
CONPLADEIN	Consejo Nacional de Planificación de los Pueblos Indígenas y Negros del Ecuador (National Planning Council for the Indigenous and Afro-Ecuadorian Peoples of Ecuador, briefly existed before being transformed into CODENPE)
DIENAZE	Dirección de Educación de la Nacionalidad Zápara del Ecuador (Administration of Education for the Zápara Nationality of Ecuador)
DINEIB	Dirección Nacional de Educación Intercultural Bilingüe (Nacional Administration of Bilingual Intercultural Education)
ECUARUNARI	Ecuador Runacunapac Riccharimui (Ecuador Indians Awaken)
FEINE	Federación de Indígenas Evangélicos del Ecuador (Federation of Evangelical Indians of Ecuador)
FEPOCAN	Federación Provincial de Organizaciones Campesinas de Napo (Provincial Federation of Peasant Organizations of Napo, which became FOIN)
FOIN	Federación de Organizaciones Indígenas del Napo (Federation of Indigenous Organizations of Napo)

IERAC	Instituto Ecuatoriano de Reforma Agraria y Colonización (Ecuadorian Institute for Agrarian Reform and Colonization, which later morphed into INDA)
ILO	International Labour Organization
IMF	International Monetary Fund
INDA	Instituto Nacional de Desarrollo Agrario (Nacional Agrarian Development Institute)
MEC	Ministerio de Educación, Cultura, Deportes, y Recreación (Ministry of Education, Culture, Sports, and Recreation)
MUPP–NP	Movimiento de Unidad Plurinacional Pachakutik–Nuevo País (Pachakutik Movement of Plurinational Unity–New Country), or Pachakutik
NASAPE	Nacionalidad Sápara de Ecuador (Zápara Nationality of Ecuador; this organization emerged out of the collapse of the Comuna Záparo)
NAZAE	Nacionalidad Zápara de Ecuador (Zápara Nationality of Ecuador, formerly ANAZPPA)
ONAZE	Organización de la Nacionalidad Záparo del Ecuador (Organization of the Záparo Nationality of Ecuador, referred to as the Comuna Záparo throughout the book to avoid confusion with NAZAE)
ONZAE	Organización de la Nacionalidad Zápara del Ecuador (Organization of the Zápara Nationality of Ecuador, which became NAZAE in 2003)
OPEC	Organization of Petroleum Exporting Countries
OPIP	Organización de Pueblos Indígenas de Pastaza (Organization of Indigenous Peoples of Pastaza)
PAEBIC	Proyecto Alternativo de Educación Bilingüe de la CONFENIAE (Alternative Project for Bilingual Education of CONFENIAE)
PEBI	Proyecto de Educación Bilingüe Intercultural (Project for Bilingual Intercultural Education)
PRODEPINE	Proyecto para el Desarrollo de los Pueblos Indígenas y Negros del Ecuador (Ecuador's Indigenous and Afro-Ecuadorian Peoples' Development Project)
UCTZE	Union de Centros de Territorio Záparo de Ecuador (Union of the Centers of the Záparo Territory of Ecuador, which later became ONAZE)
UNESCO	United Nations Educational, Scientific and Cultural Organization
UNIDAE	Universidad de las Nacionalidades Indígenas de la Amazonía Ecuatoriana (University of the Indigenous Nationalities of the Ecuadorian Amazon)

Notes

Chapter 1: Introduction

1. Kichwa is the Ecuadorian variant of Kechwa, the most widely spoken Indigenous language in the Americas (Mannheim 1991). It was the administrative language of the Inka Empire and is sometimes still spelled using Hispanic orthographic conventions: *Quichua*.

2. I draw here from Postero's (2007:13–15) comprehensive discussion of the different ways in which multiculturalism has been defined and deployed by various theorists and activists.

3. On Latin America as a whole, see Brysk 2000, Maybury-Lewis 2002, Sieder 2002, and Van Cott 2000; on Ecuador, see Pallares 2002 and Sawyer 1997.

4. See Lind 2004:62 and Sawyer 2004:93–97 for examples of the influence the World Bank and IMF had on Ecuadorian policy.

5. Excellent examples of recent works on Latin America's Indigenous struggles include Van Cott 2005, Warren and Jackson 2002, and Yashar 2005. On the emergence of Indigenous politics in Ecuador, see Clark 2005, Clark and Becker 2007, Field 1991, Macdonald 2002, Pallares 2002, and Zamosc 1994. For work on Indigenous peoples' participation in electoral politics, see Collins 2004 and Van Cott's (2005) chapter on Ecuador. Bretón 2005, North 2004, Yashar's (2005) chapter on Ecuador, and Zamosc 2004 provide important analyses of ethnic politics and neoliberal reform in Ecuador. Nelson's (1999) and Warren's (1998) works on Guatemala, Rappaport's (2005) book on Colombia, and Postero's (2007) recent study of Bolivia are important ethnographic works on Indigenous politics.

6. Suzana Sawyer's (2004) work on Organización de Pueblos Indígenas de Pastaza (OPIP) is an important example of this method of studying Indigenous politics. In framing my approach to conducting an engaged ethnography within a political movement, I have drawn from her discussion of this topic (Sawyer 2004:20–23; see also Rappaport 2005:88).

7. This convention has been used by other anthropologists working with Indigenous organizations and public figures, such as Postero (2007:20), Sawyer (2004:xiii), and Starn (1999:277).

Chapter 2: Language, History, and Zápara Identity

1. See Rubenstein's (2007:384–385) discussion of this point, as well as his list of notable exceptions, such as Whitten 1976.

2. Excellent summaries of the history of Ecuador's highland Indigenous peoples can be found in Clark and Becker 2007 and Larson 2004; an array of ethnographies also exist on the subject, such as Colloredo-Mansfeld 1999, Lyons 2006, and Weismantel 1988.

3. The 1899 law also declared Indigenous lands as "vacant," allowing merchants, miners, and traders to apply for legal title to them (Erazo 2007:185). The 1899 law was one of several passed by liberal president Eloy Alfaro (1895–1901, 1907–1911), who sought to modernize Ecuador's society and national economy. For a discussion of the contradictory effects of Alfaro's "Liberal Revolution" on Indigenous peoples, see Baud 2007, Clark 1998, and O'Connor 2007.

4. Salazar (1977) critiques the Federación Shuar and the Salesians' role in organizing it. Rubenstein (2002:167–190) provides a detailed and interesting first-person account of the formation of the Federación Shuar from healer and leader Alejandro Tsakimp.

5. Historian Kris Lane (2002:116–149) provides an intriguing discussion and analysis of Shuar resistance in the sixteenth century, using newly discovered archival records to question mythologizing by outsiders (among them, anthropologists) of certain aspects of the Shuar uprising of 1599.

Chapter 3: Zápara Leaders and Self-Representation

1. In writing about this issue among Zápara leaders, I draw from Rappaport's (2005:10–16, 23–29) discussion of Nasa Indigenous public intellectuals in Colombia. For other excellent studies of peasant and Indigenous intellectuals, see Feierman 1990, Mallon 1995, and Warren 1998.

2. Smith (1995, 1996) discusses the link between such conceptualizations of women as particularly Indigenous, and therefore antimodern, and the construction of Latin American nationalisms in the nineteenth and twentieth centuries.

3. My own research on the language confirms this, as does Andrade (2001:87).

4. Both Andrade (2001:87) and Whitten (1976:7), however, point out that the term for *basket* in Zápara is *zapáro*, not *záparo*, the stress in the Zápara language being phonemic and making a significant difference in meaning. *Záparo* was, until only recently, accepted in anthropological and historical literature, as well as government documents, as the correct spelling of *Zápara*. *Záparo* first appears in colonial accounts of the language and has been the customary way of referring to the language and the ethnicity (see Osculati 2000[1848]:223; Simson 1886:166). It may be that Záparo was a spelling that earlier Spanish-speaking priests, administrators, and travelers created to make the name agree with the masculine word *idioma* (language), therefore *el idioma Záparo*. However, I have not been able to confirm this. The issue of why the *Záparo* spelling exists is an interesting problem and requires further investigation.

5. See chapter 2 for my discussion of the Comuna Záparo and Bilhaut's (2005) work.

6. Essentialism is the idea that all cultures are constituted by a set of irreducible and unchanging core components or essences (Warren and Jackson 2002:8). The concept and its history are discussed at length in Clifford 1988.

Chapter 4: The Paradoxes of Intercultural Education

1. Several authors have explored the complex politics of gender and race in similar pageants; see Gustafson 2007, Rahier 1999, and Rogers 1998.

2. The literature on boarding schools for Indigenous children is expansive, particularly studies of the United States and Canada, which had extensive residential school systems; for a general overview of the subject, see Adams 1995, Child 1998, Lomawaima 1994, and Trafzer, Keller, and Sisquoc 2006.

3. This information comes from DIENAZE's institutional plan for 2003–2008.

4. Linguist Kendall King (1997:157–159, 2001, 2003) notes that this is a common issue among endangered-language education programs and one of the reasons—from a purely pedagogical standpoint—that these often fail to produce new speakers.

5. Paolo Freire was a Brazilian-born philosopher who developed education programs aimed at making oppressed peoples conscious of their subjugation and helping them to identify strategies for their liberation (see Freire 1970).

6. Rival (2002:171) notes similar tensions between Kichwa instructors and Waorani parents over what constitutes "work." Rival describes this tension as emanating from cultural differences between the two groups' notions of agricultural domestication and horticultural production in the rain forest.

Chapter 5: External Advocates and the Zápara UNESCO Project

1. UNESCO made proclamations in 2001, 2003, 2005, and 2009. According to the program's website (www.unesco.org/culture/ich/), applications are evaluated using the following criteria: the candidate's "roots in the cultural tradition or cultural history of the community concerned"; its "role in affirming the cultural identity of the peoples and cultural communities concerned"; its merit as a "unique testimony of living cultural traditions"; and its risk of "disappearing" because of processes of "rapid change, urbanization, or acculturation." Examples of some of the candidates chosen are the Garifuna language, dance, and music (Belize); the oral heritage of Gelede (Benin); Kuttiyatam, Sanskrit theater (India); and the Andean cosmovision of the Kallawaya (Bolivia).

2. Ecuador received one of the first World Cultural Heritage Site declarations in 1978 when Quito's colonial center was designated as such.

3. This is mirrored in the distribution of intangible heritage declarations, which are overwhelmingly concentrated in the global South—"exotic" sites that are threatened by modernity.

4. The states are Argentina (2000), Bolivia (1991), Brazil (2002), Colombia (1991), Costa Rica (1993), Dominica (2002), Ecuador (1998), Guatemala (1996), Honduras (1995), Mexico (1990), Paraguay (1993), Peru (1994), and Venezuela (2002).

5. According to Hodgson (2002:1039), the United Nations often uses the definition proposed by José Martinez Cobo, the former special rapporteur to the Subcommission on Prevention of Discrimination and Protection of Minorities, as its definition of Indigenous people:

> Indigenous communities, peoples, and nations are those which have a historical continuity with pre-invasion and pre-colonial societies that developed on their territories.... They form at present non-dominant sectors of society and are determined to

preserve, develop, and transmit to future generations their ancestral territories and their ethnic identity. (Cobo 1986:para. 379)

6. Because of this NGO's relatively small size, I have changed its name in order to further protect the identity of its workers.

7. UNESCO adopted these guidelines as the Recommendation on the Safeguarding of Traditional Culture and Folklore (see UNESCO 2003).

Chapter 6: The World Bank, Ethno-development, and Indigenous Participation

1. See my discussion of CONAIE's 2001 protest in the introduction to this book (chapter 1).

2. See, for example, the work of Putnam (2002); on social capital in development literature on Latin America, see Bebbington (1999).

3. Between 1999 and 2002, NAZAE (and its prior incarnations, ONZAE and ANAZPPA) received $164,500 from PRODEPINE, 56 percent of its overall budget of $289,096 during this period.

4. I have used a pseudonym for Jorge's organization in order to preserve his anonymity.

5. This closely mirrors the situation created by neoliberal development projects described by Lind (2005) aimed at poor Ecuadorian women during the 1990s and early 2000s. Rather than improve poor women's situations, Lind shows, women-in-development programs actually worsened them by reinforcing women's roles as unpaid providers of community services.

6. This point is argued in greater detail by Almeida Vinueza (2005).

Epilogue: Looking Back, Moving Forward

1. Apparently, Vargas channeled money to supportive communities and organizations by intentionally overpaying for community development projects. For example, Vargas is said to have allotted more than $10,000 for a chicken breeding project when the market value of the birds was just a little more than $6,000 (El Comercio 2007).

2. I owe thanks to Marc Becker for bringing Cholango's commentary to my attention.

References

Abram, Matthias
1992   El Proyecto EBI, 1985–1990: Lengua, cultura e identidad. Quito: Ediciones Abya-Yala.

Acosta, Alberto
2003   Ecuador: Entre la ilusión ỳ la maldición del petróleo. Ecuador Debate 58:77–100.

Adams, David Wallace
1995   Education for Extinction: American Indians and the Boarding School Experience, 1875–1928. Lawrence: University Press of Kansas.

Albó, Xavier
2004   Ethnic Identity and Politics in the Central Andes. *In* Politics in the Andes: Identity, Conflict, Reform. Joe-Marie Burt and Philip Mauceri, eds. Pp. 17–37. Pittsburgh: University of Pittsburgh Press.

Almeida Vinueza, José
2005   The Ecuadorian Indigenous Movement and the Gutiérrez Regime: The Traps of Multiculturalism. Political and Legal Anthropology Review 28(1):93–111.

Andrade Pallares, Carlos
2001   Kwatupama Sapara, palabra Zápara. Quito: PRODEPINE.

Baud, Michiel
2007   Liberalism, Indigenismo, and Social Mobilization in Late 19th Century Ecuador. *In* Highland Indians and the State in Modern Ecuador. A. Kim Clark and Marc Becker, eds. Pp. 72–88. Pittsburgh: University of Pittsburgh Press.

Bebbington, Anthony
1999   Capitals and Capabilities: A Framework for Analyzing Peasant Viability, Rural Livelihoods, and Poverty. World Development 27(12):2021–2044.

Becker, Marc
2003   Race, Gender, and Protest in Ecuador. *In* Work, Protest, and Identity in 20th

Century Latin America. Vincent C. Pelasco, ed. Pp. 125–142. Wilmington, DE: Scholarly Resources.

2008a   Guatemala: Americas Social Forum Rejects Neoliberalism, Celebrates Resistance. http://www.upsidedownworld.org, accessed December 1, 2008.

2008b   Indigenous Organizations to Support Ecuador's Constitution. http://upsidedownworld.org/main/content/view/1404/49/, accessed July 31, 2008.

Bilhaut, Anne-Gaël
2005   Situación de la nacionalidad Zápara y sus organizaciones: Ecuador y Perú. Unpublished MS, Département d'Ethnologie et de Sociologie Comparative, Université de Paris X Nanterre.

Bolivia
2009   Constitución política del estado.

Boston Globe
2006   White House Says Ecuador Trade Talks Stall. May 16.

Bourdieu, Pierre
1977   Outline of a Theory of Practice. New York: Cambridge University Press.
1986   The Forms of Capital. *In* Handbook for Theory and Research for the Sociology of Education. John G. Richardson, ed. Pp. 241–258. Westport, CT: Greenwood.

Bourguignon, François, Francisco H. G. Ferreira, and Nora Lustig, eds.
2004   The Microeconomics of Income Distribution Dynamics in East Asia and Latin America. Washington, DC: The World Bank.

Bretón, Víctor
2005   Capital social y etnodesarollo en los Andes. Quito: Centro Andino de Acción Popular.

Briggs, Charles
1996   The Politics of Discursive Authority in Research on the "Invention of Tradition." Cultural Anthropology 11(4):435–469.

Brysk, Alison
2000   From Tribal Village to Global Village: Indian Rights and International Relations in Latin America. Stanford, CA: Stanford University Press.
2004   From Civil Society to Collective Action: The Politics of Religion in Ecuador. *In* Resurgent Voices in Latin America: Indigenous Peoples, Political Mobilization, and Religious Change. Edward J. Cleary and Timothy J. Steigenga, eds. Pp. 25–42. New Brunswick, NJ: Rutgers University Press.

Burbano de Lara, Felipe
2005   La caída de Gutiérrez y la rebelión de abril. Íconos 9(3):19–26.

Canessa, Andrew
2005   Introduction. *In* Natives Making Nation: Gender, Indigeneity, and the State in the Andes. Andrew Canessa, ed. Pp. 3–31. Tucson: University of Arizona Press.

Carvajal, Gaspar de
1934   The Discovery of the Amazon, According to the Account of Friar Gaspar de
        Carvajal and Other Documents. Bertram E. Lee, trans. H. C. Beaton, ed. New
        York: American Geographical Society.

Centro Andino de Acción Popular (CAAP)
2003   Presupuesto general del estado y carta de intención, rinden tribute a los acree-
        dores de la deuda pública. Ecuador Debate 58:5–16.

Cepek, Michael
2008   Essential Commitments: Identity and the Politics of Cofán Conservation. Journal
        of Latin American and Caribbean Anthropology 13(1):196–222.

Child, Brenda
1998   Boarding School Seasons: American Indian Families, 1900–1940. Lincoln:
        University of Nebraska Press.

Clark, A. Kim
1994   Indians, the State, and Law: Public Works and the Struggle to Control Labor in
        Liberal Ecuador. Journal of Historical Sociology 7(1):49–72.
1998   The Redemptive Work: Railway and Nation in Ecuador, 1895–1930. Wilmington,
        DE: SR Books.
2005   Ecuadorian Indians, the Nation, and Class in a Historical Perspective: Rethinking
        a "New Social Movement." Anthropologica 47(1):53–66.

Clark, A. Kim, and Marc Becker
2007   Indigenous Peoples and State Formation in Modern Ecuador. In Highland Indians
        and the State in Modern Ecuador. A. Kim Clark and Marc Becker, eds. Pp. 1–21.
        Pittsburgh: University of Pittsburgh Press.

Cleary, David
2001   Towards an Environmental History of the Amazon: From Prehistory to the 19th
        Century. Latin American Research Review 36(2):65–96.

Clifford, James
1988   The Predicament of Culture. Cambridge, MA: Harvard University Press.
2000   Taking Identity Politics Seriously: "The Contradictory Stone Ground..." In
        Without Guarantees: In Honor of Stuart Hall. Paul Gilroy, Lawrence Grossberg,
        and Angela McRobbie, eds. Pp. 94–113. London: Verso.

Cobo, José Martinez
1986   The Study of the Problem of Discrimination against Indigenous Populations. Vols.
        1–5. New York: United Nations.

Collins, Jennifer
2004   Linking Movement and Electoral Politics. In Politics in the Andes: Identity,
        Conflict, Reform. Jo-Marie Burt and Philip Mauceri, eds. Pp. 38–57. Pittsburgh:
        University of Pittsburgh Press.

Colloredo-Mansfeld, Rudi
1999   The Native Leisure Class: Consumption and Cultural Creativity in the Andes.
        Chicago: University of Chicago Press.

Confederación de las Nacionalidades Indígenas del Ecuador (CONAIE)
2001   Resoluciones de la asamblea de la CONAIE sobre las medidas económicas. *In*
        Nada solo para los indios: El levantamiento indígena del 2001: Análisis, crónicas
        y documentos. Kintto Lucas and Leonella Cucurella, eds. Pp. 167–171. Quito:
        Ediciones Abya-Yala.

Conklin, Beth A.
1997   Body Paint, Feathers, and VCRs: Aesthetics and Authenticity in Amazonian
        Activism. American Ethnologist 24(4):711–737.

Conklin, Beth A., and Laura R. Graham
1995   The Shifting Middle Ground: Amazonian Indians and Eco-politics. American
        Anthropologist 97(4):695–710.

Costales, Piedad, and Alfredo Costales Samaniego
1975   La familia etno-lingüística Zápara. Ethos 1:3–30.

Cotacachi, Mercedes
1997   Attitudes of Teachers, Children, and Parents towards Bilingual Intercultural
        Education. *In* Indigenous Literacies in the Americas: Language Planning from the
        Bottom Up. Nancy H. Hornberger, ed. Pp. 285–298. The Hague: Mouton.

Crain, Mary
1990   The Social Construction of National Identity in Highland Ecuador.
        Anthropological Quarterly 63(1):43–59.

Crehan, Kate
2002   Gramsci, Culture, and Anthropology. Berkeley: University of California Press.

Denvir, Daniel
2008   Wayward Allies: President Rafael Correa and the Ecuadorian Left.
        https://nacla.org/node/4862, accessed July 27, 2008.

Dirección de Educación de la Nacionalidad Zápara del Ecuador (DIENAZE)
2003   Plan operativo. Unpublished MS, Puyo, Ecuador.

Ecuador
1998   Constitución Política de la Republica del Ecuador.
2008   Constitución Política de la Republica del Ecuador.

Ecuador Runacunapac Riccharimui (ECUARUNARI)
2008   Resolutions of the Extraordinary Assembly of the Confederation of the Peoples of
        the Kichwa Nationality of Ecuador. http://upsidedownworld.org/main/content/
        view/1404/49/, accessed July 31, 2008.

El Comercio
2001   Una mirada interior, etnía Zápara un patrimonio del mundo. May 20.
2004a   La dirigencia de la OPIP con cuestionamientos. July 12.
2004b   Otra polémica estalla en el CODENPE. July 15.
2007   Antonio Vargas, acusado de supuesto peculado. November 11.
2008a   Retiro de Quechua como idioma oficial molesta a Indígenas de Ecuador. July 18.
2008b   La Ecuarunari está molesta por la exclusión del Quichua. July 21.

2008c   Ecuarunari apoya el Sí pero cuestiona críticas de Correa. July 30.
2008d   La CONAIE no tiene clara su posición. August 6.
2008e   La educación bilingüe sigue relegada. August 21.

El País
2001   Al rescate de una lengua que muere, los Záparas designados patrimonio de la
          humanidad para salvar su idioma. September 27.

El Universo
2001   Etnia Zápara, patrimonio de la humanidad. May 19.

Elyachar, Julia
2002   Empowerment Money: The World Bank, Non-governmental Organizations, and
          the Value of Culture in Egypt. Public Culture 14(3):493–513.
2005   Markets of Dispossession: NGOs, Economic Development, and the State in Cairo.
          Durham, NC: Duke University Press.

Erazo, Juliet S.
2007   Same State, Different Histories, Diverse Strategies: The Ecuadorian Amazon. *In*
          Highland Indians and the State in Modern Ecuador. A. Kim Clark and Marc
          Becker, eds. Pp. 179–195. Pittsburgh: University of Pittsburgh Press.

Escobar, Arturo
1995   Encountering Development: The Making and Unmaking of the Third World.
          Princeton, NJ: Princeton University Press.

Farthing, Linda
2007   Everything Is up for Discussion: A 40th Anniversary Conversation with Silvia
          Rivera Cusicanqui. NACLA Report on the Americas 40(4):4–9.

Feierman, Steven
1990   Peasant Intellectuals: Anthropology and History in Tanzania. Madison: University
          of Wisconsin Press.

Ferguson, James
1990   The Anti-politics Machine: "Development," Depoliticization, and Bureaucratic
          Power in Lesotho. Cambridge: Cambridge University Press.
2006   Global Shadows: Africa in the Neoliberal World Order. Durham, NC: Duke
          University Press.

Field, Les
1991   Ecuador's Pan-Indian Uprising. NACLA Report on the Americas 25(3):38–44.

Fine, Ben
2001   Social Capital versus Social Theory: Political Economy and Social Science at the
          Turn of the Millennium. London: Routledge.
2003   Social Capital: The World Bank's Fungible Friend. Journal of Agrarian Change
          3(4):586–603.

Freire, Paolo
1970   Pedagogy of the Oppressed. New York: Herder and Herder.

García, María Elena

2005 Making Indigenous Citizens: Identity, Development, and Multicultural Activism in Peru. Stanford, CA: Stanford University Press.

García, María Elena, and José Antonio Lucero

2004 Un País sin Indígenas? Re-thinking Indigenous Politics in Peru. *In* The Struggle for Indigenous Rights in Latin America. Nancy Grey Postero and Léon Zamosc, eds. Pp. 158–188. Brighton [England]: Sussex Academic Press.

Geertsen, Rune

2006 Interview with Luis Macas: We Want a Total Transformation. http://upsidedownworld.org/main/content/view/433/49/, accessed July 31, 2008.

Gill, Lesley

2000 Teetering on the Rim. New York: Columbia University Press.

Graham, Laura R.

2002 How Should an Indian Speak? *In* Indigenous Movements, Self-Representation, and the State in Latin America. Kay B. Warren and Jean E. Jackson, eds. Pp. 181–228. Austin: University of Texas Press.

Gramsci, Antonio

1971a Gli intellettuali e l'organizzazione della cultura. Rome: Editori Riuniti.
1971b Selections from the Prison Notebooks. New York: International Publishers.

Grossberg, Lawrence, ed.

1996 On Postmodernism and Articulation: An Interview with Stuart Hall. *In* Stuart Hall: Critical Dialogues in Cultural Studies. David Morley and Kuan-Hsing Chen, eds. Pp. 131–150. London: Routledge.

Guerrero, Andrés

1997 The Construction of a Ventriloquist's Image: Liberal Discourse and the "Miserable Indian Race" in Late 19th Century Ecuador. Journal of Latin American Studies 29(3):555–590.

Gustafson, Bret

2002 Paradoxes of Liberal Indigenism: Indigenous Movements, State Processes, and Intercultural Reform in Bolivia. *In* The Politics of Ethnicity: Indigenous Peoples in Latin American States. David Maybury-Lewis, ed. Pp. 267–308. Cambridge, MA; London: Harvard University Press.
2007 Spectacles of Autonomy and Crisis, or, What Bulls and Beauty Queens Have to Do with Regionalism in Eastern Bolivia. Journal of Latin American and Caribbean Anthropology 11(2):351–379.

Hale, Charles R.

2002 Does Multiculturalism Menace? Governance, Cultural Rights, and the Politics of Identity in Guatemala. Journal of Latin American Studies 34(3):485–524.
2004 Rethinking Indigenous Politics in the Era of the "Indio Permitido." NACLA Report on the Americas 38(2):16–21.
2005 Neoliberal Multiculturalism: The Remaking of Cultural Rights and Racial Dominance in Central America. Political and Legal Anthropology Review 28(1):10–28.

2006   Activist Research vs. Cultural Critique: Indigenous Land Rights and the Contradictions of Politically Engaged Anthropology. Cultural Anthropology 21(1):96–120.

Harner, Michael J.
1972   The Jívaro: People of the Sacred Waterfalls. Garden City, NY: Natural History Press.

Harvey, David
2005   A Brief History of Neoliberalism. New York: Oxford University Press.

Hendricks, Janet
1991   Symbolic Counterhegemony among the Ecuadorian Shuar. *In* Nation-States and Indians in Latin America. Greg Urban and Joel Sherzer, eds. Pp. 53–71. Austin: University of Texas Press.

Hernández Castillo, R. Aída
2006   Zapastismo and the Emergence of Indigenous Feminism. *In* Dispatches from Latin America: On the Frontlines against Neoliberalism. Vijay Prashad and Teo Ballvé, eds. Pp. 229–242. Cambridge: South End Press.

Hodgson, Dorothy L.
2002   Comparative Perspectives on the Indigenous Rights Movement in Africa and the Americas. American Anthropologist 104(4):1037–1049.

Holm, Tom J., Diane Pearson, and Ben Chasis
2003   Peoplehood: A Model for the Extension of Sovereignty in American Indian Studies. Wicazo Sa Review 18(1):7–24.

Hornberger, Nancy H.
1997   Quechua Literacy and Empowerment in Peru. *In* Indigenous Literacies in the Americas: Language Planning from the Bottom Up. Nancy H. Hornberger, ed. Pp. 215–236. The Hague: Mouton.
2000   Bilingual Education Policy and Practice in the Andes: Ideological Paradox and Intercultural Possibility. Anthropology and Education Quarterly 31(2):173–201.

Hoy
1999   Una nación de 114. September 11.

Hudelson, John E.
1981   The Expansion and Development of Quichua Transitional Culture in the Upper Amazon Basin. Ph.D. dissertation, Department of Anthropology, Columbia University.
1985   The Lowland Quichua as "Tribe." *In* The Political Anthropology of Ecuador. Jeffrey Ehrenreich, ed. Pp. 59–79. Albany, NY: Society for Latin American Anthropology and the Center for the Caribbean and Latin America.

International Labor Organization (ILO)
1989   Indigenous and Tribal Peoples Convention. http://www.ilo.org/ilolex/cgi-lex/convde.pl?C169, accessed March 1, 2002.

Isaacs, Anita
1993   Military Rule and Transition in Ecuador, 1972–92. Pittsburgh: University of Pittsburgh Press.

Jackson, Jean
1991   Being and Becoming an Indian in the Vaupés. *In* Nation States and Indians in Latin America. Greg Urban and Joel Sherzer, eds. Pp. 131–155. Austin: University of Texas Press.
1995   Culture, Genuine and Spurious: The Politics of Indianess in the Vaupés, Colombia. American Ethnologist 22(1):3–27.

Jameson, William
1858   Excursion Made from Quito to the River Napo, January to May, 1857. Journal of the Royal Geographical Society 18:337–349.

Karttunnen, Frances
1994   Between Worlds: Interpreters, Guides, and Survivors. New Brunswick, NJ: Rutgers University Press.

Kimmerling, Judith
1993   Crudo Amazónico. Quito: Ediciones Abya-Yala.

King, Kendall
1997   Indigenous Politics and Native Language Literacies: Recent Shifts in Bilingual Education Policy and Practice in Ecuador. *In* Indigenous Literacies in the Americas: Language Planning from the Bottom Up. Nancy H. Hornberger, ed. Pp. 267–284. The Hague: Mouton.
2001   Language Revitalization Processes and Prospects: Quichua in the Ecuadorian Andes. Clevedon, UK: Multilingual Matters Press.
2003   Language Pedagogy and Language Revitalization: Experiences from the Ecuadorian Andes and Beyond. *In* Transcending Monolingualism: Linguistic Revitalization in Education. Leena Huss, Antoinette C. Grima, and Kendall King, eds. Pp. 149–166. Lisse; Exton, PA: Swets and Zeitlinger.

Korovkin, Tanya
1997   Indigenous Peasant Struggles and the Capitalist Modernization of Agriculture: Chimborazo, 1964–1991. Latin American Perspectives 24(3):25–49.

Lane, Kris
2002   Quito 1599. Albuquerque: University of New Mexico Press.

Larrea, Carlos, and Jeanette Sánchez
2003   Pobreza, dolarización y crisis en el Ecuador. Ecuador Debate 60:7–24.

Larson, Brooke
2004   Trials of Nation Making: Liberalism, Race, and Ethnicity in the Andes, 1810–1910. Cambridge: Cambridge University Press.

Lauer, Matthew
2006   State-Led Democratic Politics and Emerging Forms of Indigenous Leadership among the Ye'kwana of the Upper Orinoco. Journal of Latin American Anthropology 11(4):51–86.

Lazzari, Axel
2003   Aboriginal Recognition, Freedom, and Phantoms: The Vanishing of the Ranquel and the Return of the Rankulche in La Pampa. Journal of Latin American Anthropology 8(3):59–83.

León, Friar Agustín M
1937   Relación histórica de los pueblos de Santo Domingo del Tigre, de Santa Rosa del Cunambo y de San Jacinot. El Oriente Dominicana (54–55):188–193.
1938   Informe sobre las misiones del año 1912. El Oriente Dominicana (62–63):326–328.

Li, Tania Murray
2000   Articulating Indigenous Identity in Indonesia: Resource Politics and the Tribal Slot. Comparative Studies in Society and History 42(1):149–179.
2007   The Will to Improve: Governmentality, Development, and the Practice of Politics. Durham, NC: Duke University Press.

Lind, Amy
2004   Engendering Andean Politics. In Politics in the Andes: Identity, Conflict, Reform. Jo-Marie Burt and Philip Mauceri, eds. Pp. 58–80. Pittsburgh: University of Pittsburgh Press.
2005   Gendered Paradoxes: Women's Movements, State Restructuring, and Global Development in Ecuador. University Park: The Pennsylvania State University Press.

Loch, Erskine E.
1938   Fever, Famine, and Gold: The Dramatic Story of the Adventures and Discoveries of the Andes-Amazon Expedition in the Uncharted Vastness of a Lost World in the Llanganatis Mountains. New York: G. P. Putnam's Sons.

Lomawaima, Tsianina
1994   They Called It Prairie Light: The Story of Chilocco Indian School. Lincoln: University of Nebraska Press.

Lucas, Kintto
2008   New Constitution Addresses Demand for "Plurinational" State. http://www.ipsnews.net/news.asp?idnews=42235, accessed May 8, 2008.

Lucero, José Antonio
2003   Locating the "Indian Problem." Community, Nationality, and Contradiction in Ecuadorian Indigenous Politics. Latin American Perspectives 30(1):23–48.
2006a   Representing "Real Indians." The Challenges of Authenticity and Strategic Constructivism in Ecuador and Bolivia. Latin American Research Review 41(2):31–56.
2006b   Indigenous Political Voice and the Struggle for Recognition in Ecuador and Bolivia. Background Papers, World Development Report 2006: Equity and Development. http://siteresources.worldbank.org/INTWDR2006/Resources/477383-1118673432908/Indigenous_Political_Voice_and_the_Struggle_for_Recognition_in_Ecuador_and_Bolivia.pdf, accessed October 1, 2007.
2007   Barricades and Articulations: Comparing Ecuadorian and Bolivian Indigenous

Politics. *In* Highland Indians and the State in Modern Ecuador. A. Kim Clark and Marc Becker, eds. Pp. 209–233. Pittsburgh: University of Pittsburgh Press.

Luykx, Aurolyn
1999   The Citizen Factory: Schooling and Cultural Production in Bolivia. Albany: State University of New York Press.

Lyons, Barry
2006   Remembering the Hacienda: Religion, Authority, and Social Change in Highland Ecuador. Austin: University of Texas Press.

Macdonald, Theodore, Jr.
2002   Ecuador's Indian Movement: Pawn in a Short Game or Agent in State Reconfiguration? *In* The Politics of Ethnicity: Indigenous Peoples in Latin American States. David Maybury-Lewis, ed. Pp. 169–198. Cambridge, MA: Harvard University Press.

Mallon, Florencia
1995   Peasant and Nation: The Making of Postcolonial Mexico and Peru. Berkeley: University of California Press.
2005   Courage Tastes of Blood: The Mapuche Community of Nicholás Ailío and the Chilean State, 1906–2001. Durham, NC: Duke University Press.

Mannheim, Bruce
1991   The Language of the Inka since the European Invasion. Austin: University of Texas Press.

Martin, Pamela L.
2003   The Globalization of Contentious Politics: The Amazonian Indigenous Rights Movement. New York: Routledge.

Martz, John D.
1987   Politics and Petroleum in Ecuador. New Brunswick, NJ: Transaction Books.

Maybury-Lewis, David, ed.
2002   The Politics of Ethnicity: Indigenous Peoples in Latin American States. Cambridge, MA: Harvard University Press.

Moya, Ruth
1990   A Decade of Bilingual Education and Indigenous Participation in Ecuador. Prospects 20(3):331–343.

Muratorio, Blanca
1991   The Life and Times of Grandfather Alonso: Culture and History in the Upper Amazon. New Brunswick, NJ: Rutgers University Press.
1998   Indigenous Women's Identities and the Politics of Cultural Reproduction in the Ecuadorian Amazon. American Anthropologist 100(2):409–420.

Nacionalidad Zápara de Ecuador (NAZAE)
2001a   Candidatura para la proclamación de obras maestras del patrimonio oral y herencia intangible de la humanidad. Unpublished MS, NAZAE, Puyo, Ecuador.

2001b   Boletín de prensa: La tradición oral de los indígenas Záparas, reconocida por
         UNESCO como patrimonio inmaterial de la humanidad. News release, NAZAE,
         Puyo, Ecuador.
2003   Mapa del territorio. Unpublished MS, NAZAE, Puyo, Ecuador.

Nelson, Diane
1999   A Finger in the Wound: Body Politics in Quincentennial Guatemala. Berkeley:
         University of California Press.

North, Liisa
2004   State Building, State Dismantling, and Financial Crises in Ecuador. In Politics in
         the Andes: Identity, Conflict, Reform. Joe-Marie Burt and Philip Mauceri, eds.
         Pp. 187–206. Pittsburgh: University of Pittsburgh Press.

Oakdale, Suzanne
2004   The Culture-Conscious Brazilian Indian: Representing and Reworking Indianness
         in Kayabi Political Discourse. American Ethnologist 31(1):60–75.

Obrerem, Udo
1974   Trade and Trade Goods in the Ecuadorian Montaña. In Native South Americans:
         Ethnology of the Least Known Continent. Patricia J. Lyon, ed. Pp. 347–357.
         Boston: Little, Brown.

O'Connor, Erin
2007   Helpless Children or Undeserving Patriarchs? Gender Ideologies, the State, and
         Indian Men in Late 19th-Century Ecuador. In Highland Indians and the State in
         Modern Ecuador. A. Kim Clark and Marc Becker, eds. Pp. 56–71. Pittsburgh:
         University of Pittsburgh Press.

Orton, James
1876   The Andes and the Amazon, or, Across the Continent of South America. New
         York: Harper.

Osculati, Gaetano
2000   Exploración de las regiones ecuatoriales a través del Napo y de los ríos de las
[1848]   Amazonas. Quito: Ediciones Abya-Yala.

Pallares, Amalia
2002   From Peasant Struggles to Indian Resistance: The Ecuadorian Andes in the Late
         Twentieth Century. Norman: University of Oklahoma Press.

Parandekar, Suhas, Rob Vos, and Donald Winkler
2002   Ecuador: Crisis, Poverty, and Social Protection. In Crisis and Dollarization in
         Ecuador. Paul E. Beckerman and Andrés Solimano, eds. Pp. 127–176.
         Washington, DC: World Bank.

Peeke, Catherine
1962   Structural Summary of Záparo. In Studies in Ecuadorian Indian Languages.
         Benjamin Elson, ed. Pp. 125–216. Norman: Summer Institute of the Linguistics
         of the University of Oklahoma.
1991   Bosquejo grammatical del Záparo. Revised by Mary Ruth Wise and Stephen H.
         Levinson. Cuadernos Ethnolingüísticos 14. Quito: Instituto Lingüístico de Verano.

Pierre, François
1988 Voyage d'exploration d'un missionaire Dominican chez lez tribus sauvage de
[1889] L'Equateur. Quito: Ediciones Abya-Yala.

Ponce, Juan
2004 Etnicidad y educación en el Ecuador. Paper presented at the 8th Ecuadorian
Congress of Sociology and Latin American Meeting of Social Sciences, Quito, July
26–29.

Postero, Nancy Grey
2007 Now We Are Citizens: Indigenous Politics in Postmulticultural Bolivia. Stanford,
CA: Stanford University Press.

**Proyecto para el Desarrollo de los Pueblos Indígenas y Negros del Ecuador
(PRODEPINE)**
2002 Informe de cierre del proyecto de desarollo de los pueblos Indígenas y Negros del
Ecuador. Quito: PRODEPINE.
N.d. Pautas metodológicas del programa de patrimonio cultural. Unpublished working
document, PRODEPINE, Quito.

Psacharapolous, George, and Harry Anthony Patrinos
1994 Indigenous Peoples and Poverty in Latin America: An Empirical Analysis.
Washington, DC: World Bank.

Putnam, Robert D.
2002 Foreword. In The Role of Social Capital in Development: An Empirical
Assessment. Christian Grootaert and Thierry van Bastelaer, eds. Pp. xxi–xxiii.
Cambridge, MA: Harvard University Press.

Radcliffe, Sarah A.
2001 Imagining the State as Space: Territoriality and the Formation of the State in
Ecuador. In States of Imagination: Ethnographic Explorations of the Postcolonial
State. Thomas B. Hansen and Finn Stepputat, eds. Pp. 123–145. Durham, NC:
Duke University Press.
2002 Indigenous Women, Rights, and the Nation-State in the Andes. In Gender and the
Politics of Rights and Democracy in Latin America. Nikki Craske and Maxine
Molyneux, eds. Pp. 149–172. New York: Palgrave.

Radcliffe, Sarah, and Sally Westwood
1996 Remaking the Nation: Place, Identity, and Politics in Latin America. London:
Routledge.

Rahier, Jean Muteba
1999 Blackness, the Racial/Spatial Order, Migrations, and Miss Ecuador 1995–96.
American Anthropologist 100(2):421–430.

Ramos, Alcida
1998 Indigenism: Ethnic Politics in Brazil. Madison: University of Wisconsin Press.

Rappaport, Joanne
2005 Intercultural Utopias: Public Intellectuals, Cultural Experimentation, and Ethnic
Pluralism in Colombia. Durham, NC: Duke University Press.

Reeve, Mary-Elizabeth

1988a   Los Quichuas del Curaray, el proceso de formación de la identidad. Quito: Ediciones Abya-Yala.

1988b   Cauchu Uras: Lowland Quichua Histories of the Amazon Rubber Boom. *In* Rethinking History and Myth: Indigenous South American Perspectives on the Past. Jonathan D. Hill, ed. Pp. 19–34. Urbana: University of Illinois Press.

Rival, Laura

2002   Trekking through History: The Huaorani of Amazonian Ecuador. New York: Columbia University Press.

Rivera Cusicanqui, Silvia

2008   Colonialism and Ethnic Resistance in Bolivia: A View from the Coca Markets. *In* Empire and Dissent: The United States and Latin America. Fred Rosen, ed. Pp. 137–161. Durham, NC: Duke University Press.

Rogers, Mark

1998   Spectacular Bodies: Folklorization and the Politics of Identity in Ecuadorian Beauty Pageants. Journal of Latin American Anthropology 3(2):54–85.

Rose, Nikolas

1999   Powers of Freedom: Reframing Political Thought. Cambridge: Cambridge University Press.

Roseberry, William

1994   Hegemony and the Language of Contention. *In* Everyday Forms of State Formation: Revolution and the Negotiation of Rule in Modern Mexico. Gilbert M. Joseph and Daniel Nugent, eds. Pp. 355–366. Durham, NC: Duke University Press.

Rubenstein, Steven

2002   Alejandro Tsakimp: A Shuar Healer on the Margins of History. Lincoln: University of Nebraska Press.

2007   Circulation, Accumulation, and the Power of Shuar Shrunken Heads. Cultural Anthropology 22(3):357–399.

Salazar, Ernesto

1977   An Indian Federation in Lowland Ecuador: Document 28. Copenhagen: International Work Group for Indigenous Affairs.

Sawyer, Suzana

1997   Marching to Nation across Ethnic Terrain: The 1992 Indian Mobilization in Lowland Ecuador. Latin American Perspectives 24(3):65–82.

2004   Crude Chronicles: Indigenous Politics, Multinational Oil, and Neoliberalism in Ecuador. Durham, NC: Duke University Press.

Selverston-Scher, Melina

2001   Ethnopolitics in Ecuador: Indigenous Rights and the Strengthening of Democracy. Miami: North–South Center Press.

Shepherd, Chris J.

2004   Agricultural Hybridity and the "Pathology" of Traditional Ways: The Translation of Desire and Need in Postcolonial Development. Journal of Latin American Anthropology 9(2):235–266.

Sieder, Rachel, ed.
2002   Multiculturalism in Latin America: Indigenous Rights, Diversity, and Democracy. New York: Palgrave Macmillan.

Simson, Alfred
1886   Travels in the Wilds of Ecuador and the Exploration of the Putumayo River. London: Simpson, Low, Marston, Searle, and Rivington.

Slater, Candace
2004   Entangled Edens: Visions of the Amazon. Berkeley: University of California Press.

Smith, Carol A.
1995   Race-Class-Gender Ideology in Guatemala: Modern and Anti-modern Forms. Comparative Studies in Society and History 37(4):723–749.
1996   Myths, Intellectuals, and Race/Class/Gender Distinctions in the Formation of Latin American Nations. Journal of Latin American Anthropology 2(1):148–169.

Speed, Shannon
2006a   Rights at the Intersection: Gender and Ethnicity in Neoliberal Mexico. In Dissident Women: Gender and Cultural Politics in Chiapas. Shannon Speed, R. Aida Hernandez Castilla, and Lynn M. Stephen, eds. Pp. 203–221. Austin: University of Texas Press.
2006b   At the Crossroads of Human Rights and Anthropology: Toward a Critically Engaged Activist Research. American Anthropologist 108(1):66–76.

Stanfield, Michael E.
1998   Red Rubber, Bleeding Trees: Violence, Slavery, and Empire in Northwest Amazonia, 1850–1933. Albuquerque: University of New Mexico Press.

Stark, Louisa R.
1981   La lengua Zapara del Ecuador. Miscelánea Antropológica Ecuatoriana 1:12–91.

Starn, Orin
1999   Nightwatch: The Politics of Practice in the Andes. Durham, NC: Duke University Press.

Steward, Julian H., and Alfred Métraux
1948   Tribes of the Peruvian and Ecuadorian Montaña. In The Handbook of South American Indians. Julian Steward, ed. Pp. 628–651. Bureau of American Ethnology 143, no. 3. Washington, DC: Smithsonian Institution.

Striffler, Steve
2002   In the Shadows of State and Capital: The United Fruit Company, Popular Struggle, and Agrarian Restructuring in Ecuador, 1900–1995. Durham, NC: Duke University Press.

Taussig, Michael
1987   Shamanism, Colonialism, and the Wild Man: A Study in Terror and Healing. Chicago: University of Chicago Press.

Taylor, Anne-Christine
1981   God-Wealth: The Achuar and the Missions. *In* Cultural Transformations and Ethnicity in Modern Ecuador. Norman E. Whitten, ed. Pp. 647–676. Urbana: University of Illinois Press.
1999   The Western Margins of Amazonia from the Early Sixteenth to the Early Nineteenth Century. *In* The Cambridge History of Native Peoples of the Americas, vol. 3: South America, Part 2. Frank Salomon and Stewart B. Schwarz, eds. Pp. 188–256. Cambridge: Cambridge University Press.

Taylor, Charles
1994   The Politics of Recognition. *In* Multiculturalism: Examining the Politics of Recognition. Amy Gutman, ed. Pp. 25–73. Princeton, NJ: Princeton University Press.

Tessman, Gunter
1999   Los Indígenas del Peru nororiental. Quito: Ediciones Abya-Yala.
[1930]

Tilley, Virginia Q.
2002   New Help or New Hegemony? The Transnational Indigenous People's Movement and "Being Indian" in El Salvador. Journal of Latin American Studies 34(3):525–554.
2005   Seeing Indians: A Study of Race, Nation, and Power in El Salvador. Albuquerque: University of New Mexico Press.

Torres, Rosa María
2005   Real Options for Policy and Practice in Ecuador. Background Papers: All Global Monitoring Report, UNESCO. http://unesdoc.unesco.org/images/0014/001461/146190e.pdf, accessed March 5, 2008.

Trafzer, Clifford, Jean A. Keller, and Lorenc Sisquoc, eds.
2006   Boarding School Blues: Revisiting American Indian Educational Experiences. Lincoln: University of Nebraska Press.

Treakle, Kay
1998   Ecuador: Structural Adjustment and Indigenous and Environmentalist Resistance. *In* The Struggle for Accountability: The World Bank, NGOs, and Grassroots Movements. Jonathan Fox and L. David Brown, eds. Pp. 217–263. Cambridge, MA: MIT Press.

Trujillo, Jorge Nelson
2001   Memorias del Curaray. Quito: Fondo Ecuatoriano Populorum Progressio.

Tsing, Anna Lowenhaupt
2005   Friction: An Ethnography of Global Connection. Princeton, NJ: Princeton University Press.

Turner, Terence
1991   Representing, Resisting, Rethinking: Historical Transformations of Kayapó Culture and Anthropological Consciousness. *In* Colonial Situations: Essays on the Contextualization of Ethnographic Knowledge. George Stocking, ed. Pp. 285–313. Madison: University of Wisconsin Press.

United Nations (UN)
2007   United Nations Declaration on the Rights of Indigenous Peoples.
        http://www.un.org/ esa/socdev/unpfii/en/declaration.html, accessed February 24,
        2009.

United Nations Educational, Scientific and Cultural Organization (UNESCO)
2003   Convention for the Safeguarding of the Intangible Cultural Heritage.
        http://portal.unesco.org/en/ev.php-URL_ID=17716&URL_DO=DO_TOPIC&URL_
        SECTION=201.html, accessed April 15, 2004.

Uquillas, Jorge E.
1984   Colonization and Spontaneous Settlement in the Ecuadorian Amazon. In Frontier
        Expansion in Amazonia. Marianne Schmink and Charles H. Wood, eds. Pp.
        261–284. Gainesville: University of Florida Press.

Uquillas, Jorge E., and Pilar Larreamendy
2006   Applied Anthropology in Ecuador: Development, Practice, and Discourse. NAPA
        Bulletin 25:14–34.

Ushigua, Luciano
2006   Tsitsanu. Quito: Kuri Ashpa.

Uzendoski, Michael
2005   The Napo Runa of Amazonian Ecuador. Urbana-Champaign: University of Illinois
        Press.

Van Cott, Donna Lee
2000   The Friendly Liquidation of the Past: The Politics of Diversity in Latin America.
        Pittsburgh: University of Pittsburgh Press.
2005   From Movements to Parties in Latin America: The Evolution of Ethnic Politics.
        Cambridge: Cambridge University Press.
2006   Multiculturalism versus Neoliberalism in Latin America. In Multiculturalism and
        the Welfare State. Keith Banting and Will Kymlicka, eds. Pp. 272–296. Oxford:
        Oxford University Press.

Van den Berg, Maarten H. J.
2003   Mainstreaming Ethnodevelopment: Poverty and Ethnicity in World Bank Policy.
        Research of International Social Questions Papers. http://www.risq.org/
        article17.html, accessed June 2, 2004.

Van Nieuwkoop, Marten, and Jorge E. Uquillas
2000   Defining Ethnodevelopment in Operational Terms: Lessons from the Ecuador
        Indigenous and Afro-Ecuadorian Peoples Project. LCR Sustainable Development
        Working Paper 6. Washington, DC: World Bank.

Varese, Stefano
2002   Salt of the Mountain: Campa Asháninka History and Resistance in the Peruvian
        Jungle. Norman: University of Oklahoma Press.

Vargas, Friar José María
1937   Pueblos de la mision Dominicana de Canelos. El Oriente Dominicana (47):38–39.

Velasco Abad, Fernando
1983   Reforma agraria y movimiento campesino Indígena de la Sierra. Quito: Editorial
        El Conejo.

Viatori, Maximilian
2007   Zápara Leaders and Identity Construction in Ecuador: The Complexities of
        Indigenous Self-Representation. Journal of Latin American and Caribbean
        Anthropology 12(1):104–133.

Warren, Kay B.
1998   Indigenous Movements and Their Critics, Pan-Maya Activism in Guatemala.
        Princeton, NJ: Princeton University Press.

Warren, Kay B., and Jean E. Jackson, eds.
2002   Indigenous Movements, Self-Representation, and the State in Latin America.
        Austin: University of Texas Press.
2005   Indigenous Movements in Latin America, 1992–2004: Controversies, Ironies, New
        Directions. Annual Review of Anthropology 34:549–573.

Washington Post
2006   Ecuador Mobilizing to Curb Indian Protests. March 22.
2007   In Bolivia, Speaking Up for Native Languages. January 30.

Waters, William
2007   Indigenous Communities, Landlords, and the State: Land and Labor in Highland
        Ecuador, 1950–1975. In Highland Indians and the State in Modern Ecuador.
        A. Kim Clark and Marc Becker, eds. Pp. 120–138. Pittsburgh: University of
        Pittsburgh Press.

Weismantel, Mary
1988   Food, Gender, and Poverty in the Ecuadorian Andes. Philadelphia: University of
        Pennsylvania Press.
2001   Cholas and Pishtacos: Stories of Race and Sex in the Andes. Chicago: University
        of Chicago Press.

Whitten, Norman E.
1976   Sacha Runa: Ethnicity and Adaptation of Ecuadorian Jungle Quichua. Urbana:
        University of Illinois Press.

Whitten, Norman E., Dorothea Scott Whitten, and Alfonso Chango
1997   Return of the Yumbo: The Indigenous Caminata from Amazonia to Andean Quito.
        American Ethnologist 24(2):355–391.

Wilson, Fiona
2001   In the Name of the State? Schools and Teachers in an Andean Province. In
        States of Imagination: Ethnographic Explorations of the Postcolonial State.
        Thomas B. Hansen and Finn Stepputat, eds. Pp. 313–344. Durham, NC: Duke
        University Press.

Wise, Mary Ruth
1999   Small Language Families and Isolates in Peru. In The Amazonian Languages.

Robert M. W. Dixon and Alexandra Y. Aikhenvald, eds. Pp. 307–340. Cambridge: Cambridge University Press.

Wogan, Peter
2004   Magical Writing in Salasaca: Literacy and Power in Highland Ecuador. Boulder, CO: Westview.

World Bank
1995a   Ecuador Poverty Report. Washington, DC: World Bank.
1995b   Ecuador: Indigenous Peoples Development Project. Project Information Document. Washington, DC: World Bank.
1997   Ecuador: Indigenous and Afro-Ecuadorian Peoples Project. Project Appraisal Document. Washington, DC: World Bank.
1999   Ecuador: Country Assistance Evaluation. Operations Evaluation Department Document. Washington, DC: World Bank.

Yánez Cossío, Consuelo
1995   La educación Indígena en el Ecuador: Historia de la educación y el pensamiento pedagógico ecuatoriano. Quito: Ediciones Abya-Yala.

Yashar, Deborah J.
2005   Contesting Citizenship in Latin America: The Rise of Indigenous Movements and the Postliberal Challenge. Cambridge: Cambridge University Press.

Zamosc, Leon
1994   Agrarian Protest and the Indian Movement in the Ecuadorian Highlands. Latin American Research Review 29(3):37–68.
2004   The Indian Movement in Ecuador: From Politics of Influence to Politics of Power. *In* The Struggle for Indigenous Rights in Latin America. Nancy Grey Postero and Leon Zamosc, eds. Pp. 131–157. Brighton [England]: Sussex Academic Press.

Index

Chuji, Monica, 76
class, formal education and knowledge of
Spanish as indicators of, 73
Clifford, James, 127n6
Cobo, José Martinez, 128n5
CODENPE. *See* Consejo de Desarrollo de
las Nacionalidades y Pueblos del
Ecuador
Cofán (Ecuador), 32
Colombia, 25, 53–54, 96
colonialism and colonization, in Amazon
between 1964 and 1994, 29. *See also*
Spain
Comuna Záparo (Záparo Commune), 11,
33–34, 49–52, 106, 118
community: DIENAZE's education program
and schools in, 65–66, 68–75; PRODE-
PINE and community-directed self-
analysis, 107, 112
CONAIE. *See* Confederación de las
Nacionalidades Indígenas del Ecuador
Conambo River (Ecuador), 15, *16*, 34
Confederación de Nacionalidades Indígenas
de la Amazonía Ecuatoriana
(Confederation of Indigenous
Nationalities of the Ecuadorian
Amazon, CONFENIAE): 31–32, 38,
62, 64, 98, 118
Confederación de las Nacionalidades
Indígenas del Ecuador (Confederation
of Indigenous Nationalities of Ecuador,
CONAIE): and Indigenous education,
75–76; and national mobilization in
2001, 4; and opposition to policies of
World Bank, 9, 98; and PRODEPINE,
103–104, 111; status of after 2000,
117, 118–119
CONFENIAE. *See* Confederación de las
Nacionalidades Indígenas del Ecuador
Conklin, Beth A., 48, 84
Consejo de Dessarrollo de las
Nacionalidades y Pueblos del Ecuador
(Development Council of the
Nationalities and Peoples of Ecuador,
CODENPE), 99–113, 118, 120
Consejo Nacional de Planificación de los
Pueblos Indígenas y Negros del
Ecuador (National Planning Council for

the Indigenous and Afro-Ecuadorian
Peoples of Ecuador, CONPLADEIN),
104
constitution, of Ecuador: and plurinationalism, 119–120; and right to universal
education, 77; and right of Indigenous
peoples to bilingual education, 63
Correa, Rafael, 77, 119
Cueva, Padre, 21
cultural heritage, and UNESCO, 80–83
Culture of Peace program (UNESCO), 82
Cuyacocha (community), 34

Declaration on the Rights of Indigenous
Peoples (2007), 80–81
Democratic Left Party, 64
development. *See* economics
DIENAZE. *See* Dirección de Educación de
la Nacionalidad Zápara del Ecuador
DINEIB. *See* Dirección Nacional de
Educación Intercultural Bilingüe
Dirección de Educación Bilingüe de Pastaza
(Administration of Bilingual Education
in Pastaza), 55
Dirección de Educación de la Nacionalidad
Zápara del Ecuador (Administration of
Education for the Zápara Nationality of
Ecuador, DIENAZE), 64–68, 69, 71,
74, 75, 112, 120
Dirección Nacional de Educación
Intercultural Bilingüe (National
Administration of Bilingual
Intercultural Education, DINEIB),
62–63, 64, 65
dirigentes (leaders). *See* leaders and leader-
ship
diseases: and rubber boom, 25; and
Spanish colonial period in Ecuador,
19–20, 22
Dominicans, 25, 29. *See also* missionaries

economics: and impact of development
projects on women, 129n5; neoliberalism and financial crisis in Ecuador in
2001, 4, 7–8; World Bank and
Indigenous participation in development, 81, 98–113
Ecuador: and borrowing of funds to benefit

Indigenous population, 99; colonization and Indigenous organization in Amazonian, 27–32; economic crisis and national mobilization of protest in 2001, 4; education and multiculturalism in, 55–77; elites and view of Indigenous identity in, 4; history of Indigenous peoples of, 2; and independence, 22; neoliberalism and Indigenous rights in, 4–9; NGOs in Amazonian, 84; restrictions on multiculturalism from 2003 to present, 117–120; and Special Law of the Oriente (1899), 24; and status of Zápara as Indigenous nationality, 1–2; and World Bank's 1999 Country Assistance Evaluation Report, 102; as World Cultural Heritage Site, 128n2. *See also* Amazon and Amazonian peoples; constitution; Kichwa; Shuar; Waorani; Zápara

ECUARUNARI (Ecuador Runacunapac Riccharimui or Ecuador Indians Awaken), 76, 117, 119

education: and multiculturalism in Ecuador, 55–77; PRODEPINE and funding of Zápara, 106–107, 109; of Zápara dirigentes, 40. *See also* bilingual education; boarding schools; literacy; teachers

El Comercio (newspaper), 1, 76

El País (newspaper), 44

El Salvador, 82

El Universo (newspaper), 1

Elyachar, Julia, 102

encomiendas (royal estates), 19, 20–21

Erazo, Juliet S., 19, 30–31, 32

Escuelas Radiofónicas (Radio Schools), 61

"expert," role of in preservation of Zápara culture, 91, 92–93. *See also* advocates

family, and politics in treatment of elders by Zápara leaders, 48

Farthing, Linda, 42

Federación Indígenas Evangélicas del Ecuador (FEINE), 119

Federación de Organizaciones Indígenas del Napo (Federation of Indigenous

Organizations of Napo, FOIN), 31

Federación Provincial de Organizaciones de Napo (Provincial Federation of Peasant Organizations of Napo, FEPOCAN), 31

Federación Shuar (Shuar Federation), 30, 61, 127n4. *See also* Shuar

festival, and Indigenous culture in Puyo, 55–57

Fine, Ben, 100–101

Franciscans, 59. *See also* missionaries

Freire, Paolo, 128n5

Gae (Ecuador), 24

García, María Elena, 57–58, 74

García Moreno, Gabriel, 59

gender: politics of NAZAE and Zápara social discourse, 42; politics of and teachers in Zápara communities, 71; and treatment of elders by Zápara leaders, 48. *See also* women

Graham, Laura R., 43, 46, 48, 84

Gramsci, Antonio, 40

grant proposals, and non-Indigenous advocates for Zápara organizations, 87–88, 109, 122

Gutiérrez, Lucio, 64, 117, 118

hacienda system, 19

Hale, Charles R., 5, 53

Hendricks, Janet, 44

Hodgson, Dorothy L., 38, 83, 128n5

identity: history of Zápara language and, 15–36; Indigenous activists and representation of Zápara, 39–43; and Indigenous education in Latin America, 58–64; and self-identification in international declarations on Indigenous rights, 81; shamanism and revival of Zápara, 89

Indígenas, use of term, 14, 28–29

Indigenous peoples: colonization in Amazon region and organization of, 27–32; debate on use of terms in anthropology and Indigenous studies, 14; and development policies of World Bank, 101–103; historical division of into *auca* (wild) and *manso* (tame),

literacy: and Indigenous education in Ecuador, 59, 61; Zápara and community education, 68–69

Llanchamacocha (community), 34, 71, 73, 121

Loja (province), 113

Lucero, José Antonio, 9, 35, 103, 104, 113

Macas, Luis, 117, 119

Macdonald, Theodore, 35

Mahuad, Jamil, 7, 104

manso (tame), 23–24

Martin, Pamela L., 84

Martz, John D., 26

Masterpieces of the Oral and Intangible Heritage of Humanity program. *See* UNESCO

Mazaramu (community), 34

MEC. *See* Ministerio de Educación, Cultura, Deportes y Recreación

Mexico, 6

Ministerio Bienstar Social (Ministry of Social Welfare), 118

Ministerio de Educación, Cultura, Deportes y Recreación (Ministry of Education, Culture, Sports and Recreation, MEC), 3–4, 63, 64, 66

missionaries: and history of Ecuadorian Amazon, 19–24; and Indigenous education in Ecuador, 59, 61; and Zápara leaders, 50. *See also* Dominicans; Franciscans; Jesuits; Salesians

Model for Intercultural Bilingual Education (Ministry of Education and Culture, 1993), 63

Morales, Evo, 76

multiculturalism: Ecuador and restrictions on officially endorsed from 2003 to present, 117; and perspectives on reforms in Central America, 5–6, 8–9. *See also* official multiculturalism; plurinationalism

Muratorio, Blanca, 19, 21, 26, 27, 48, 61

Nacionalidad Sápara de Ecuador (Zápara Nationality of Ecuador, NASAPE), 120

Nahua (El Salvador), 82

Nasa (Colombia), 53–54

National Culture Law of 1972, 29

Nationalidad Zápara de Ecuador (Zápara Nationality of Ecuador, NAZAE): and administration of Zápara education, 58, 75; changes in after 2004, 116–123; CODENPE and recognition of Zápara as nationality, 106; establishment of, 2, 34; and exploitation of openings created by official multicultural reforms, 10–11; and identity of Zápara leaders, 39–43; methodology of ethnic research with, 13–14; non-Indigenous advocates and UNESCO project, 78–79, 83–89, 91–97; participation of in PRODE-PINE, 100, 106, 107–113, 129n3; and public protest in Puyo in 2003, 37; relations between Zápara communities and leaders of, 71–72, 73–74; and revitalization of Zápara language, 75; role of women in, 41–43; tension between leaders of Comuna Záparo and, 49–52; and UNESCO recognition of Zápara cultural identity, 3, 50, 78–79, 83–89, 91–97. *See also* Zápara

nationality. *See* identity; Indigenous peoples; plurinationalism; Zápara

NAZAE. *See* Nationalidad Zápara de Ecuador

Nelson, Diane, 126n5

neoliberalism: and autonomous Indigenous education, 62–63; and impact of development programs on women, 129n5; and Indigenous rights in Ecuador, 4–9; use of term, 6

NGOs (nongovernmental organizations): and environmental and human rights campaigns in Ecuadorian Amazon, 84; and funding for Indigenous projects, 9; and Indigenous development, 9, 101, 109–110, 112

Noboa, Gustavo, 4

Oakdale, Suzanne, 49

Occidental Oil, 119

O'Connor, Erin, 59

official multiculturalism: and focus of ethnographic study of Zápara nationality, 10–12; use of term, 5

oil industry: and free trade agreements,

119; and government land titles in Pastaza province, 33; and history of Ecuador, 25–27; and Indigenous responses to colonization in Amazon, 29

OPIP. *See* Organización de Pueblos Indígenas de Pastaza

Oral Heritage and Cultural Manifestations award (UNESCO), 80

Orellana, Francisco, 19

organic intellectuals, Zápara leaders and concept of, 40

Organización de la Nacionalidad Záparo del Ecuador (Organization of the Záparo Nationality of Ecuador, ONAZE). *See* Comuna Záparo

Organización de Pueblos Indígenas de Pastaza (Organization of Indigenous Peoples of Pastaza, OPIP), 31, 32–33, 37, 51, 118, 126n6

Orton, James, 22–23

Osculati, Gaetano, 22, 23

Pacayacu (community), 70

Paez, Federico, 26

Palacio, Alfredo, 118, 119

Pastaza (province), 32

pedagogy, training of Zápara teachers and models of, 66–68, 69

performance: Indigenous spokespeople and Zápara activism, 38–39; family networks and gender discourses of Zápara leaders, 48

Peru, 25, 57–58, 74

PetroEcuador, 119

Pierre, François, 23

Pizarro, Gonzalo, 19

Plan de Vida Zápara (Zápara Livelihood Plan), 121

plurinationalism: and concept of nationality in Amazonian Ecuador, 35; Indigenous organizations and concept of Ecuadorian nation-state, 8, 119–120; use of term, 5. *See also* Multiculturalism

politics: neoliberalism and crisis of representation and state legitimacy in Ecuador, 8; and representations of

Ecuadorian nationalism in Zápara schools, 66; Zápara activism and redefinition of Ecuadorian, 123. *See also* constitution; gender; neoliberalism

Postero, Nancy Grey, 5–6, 126n2, 126n5

Princesa Indígena de Pastaza (Indigenous Princess of Pastaza) competition, 56–57, 58

PRODEPINE. *See* Proyecto para el Desarrollo de los Pueblos Indígenas y Negros del Ecuador

Proyecto Alternativo de Educación Bilingüe de la CONFENIAE (Alternative Project for Bilingual Education of CONFENIAE, PAEBIC), 62

Proyecto para el Desarrollo de los Pueblos Indígenas y Negros del Ecuador (Ecuador's Indigenous and Afro-Ecuadorian Peoples' Development Project, PRODEPINE), 99–113, 128n3

Puyo (town), 55–57

Quechua language (Bolivia), 76

Quichua. *See* Kichwa

Radcliffe, Sarah A., 28, 42

radio stations: and Indigenous education, 61; and PRODEPINE, 106

Rappaport, Joanne, 43, 53–54, 79, 96, 126n5, 127n1

reducciones (settlements), 19, 20–21

Reina de Puyo (Queen of Puyo) competition, 55–57, 58

religion. *See* missionaries

representation. *See* leaders and leadership; self-representation

resistance, of Indigenous peoples to colonialism in Ecuador, 21, 127n5

Rival, Laura, 128n6

Roseberry, William, 9

Royal Dutch Shell. *See* Shell Oil

rubber industry, and history of Amazon and Amazonian peoples, 24–25

Rubenstein, Steven, 18, 127n1, 127n4

Salazar, Ernesto, 127n4

Salesians, 29–30, 61, 127n4. *See also* missionaries

San Javier de los Gayes (mission), 21
Santi, Marlon, 75–76
Sarayaku (Kichwa community), 32, 37
Sawyer, Suzana, 8, 26, 31, 33, 126n6
schools. *See* community; education
second-tier organizations, and Indigenous
    development, 104–105, 113
self-representation, Zápara leaders and
    strategies of, 43–49
Selverston-Scher, Melina, 62
Semigae (Ecuador), 24
shamanism: and cultural identity of
    Colombian Nasa activists, 53; and
    revival of Zápara identity, 89
Sheikh Zayed Bin Sultan al Nahyan Prize,
    92
Shell Oil, 25–27
Shuar: and Indigenous organization in
    Amazon, 29–31; language and self-rep-
    resentation of leaders, 44; missionaries
    and boarding schools, 61; and official
    use of Indigenous languages, 77; and
    resistance to Spanish colonialism, 21,
    127n5. *See also* Federación Shuar
Simson, Alfred, 23
slavery, and rubber traders, 24, 25
Smith, Carol A., 127n2
social capital, and development policies of
    World Bank, 100–101, 107, 112, 113
solidarios. See advocates
Spain: and history of Ecuador, 19–24; non-
    Indigenous advocates and international
    solidarity campaigns based in, 85. *See
    also* colonialism and colonization
Spanish language: cultural authenticity and
    use of by Zápara, 52; and NAZAE diri-
    gentes, 41, 52; as official language in
    Ecuadorian constitution, 77; and oil
    industry, 26; Zápara and Indigenous
    education, 64–69
Speed, Shannon, 5–6
Stanfield, Michael E., 24
Starn, Orin, 18, 97
Striffler, Steve, 9
Summer Institute of Linguistics, 25

Taylor, Anne-Christine, 20, 21, 22
teachers; status of in Zápara communities,

71–72; Zápara schools and training of,
    66–68, 69. *See also* education
tierras baldías (barren or uninhabited land),
    27–28
Tilley, Virginia Q., 80, 81–82
traders, and history of Amazonian peoples
    of Ecuador, 24–25
"Transnational Indigenous Peoples
    Movement," 80
Tsakimp, Alejandro, 127n4
Tsing, Anna Lowenhaupt, 90–91, 97
Tsitsano (creation figure), 47

Union de Centros de Territorio Záparo del
    Ecuador (Union of the Centers of the
    Záparo Territory of Ecuador, UCTZE),
    33
United Nations: and definition of
    Indigenous people, 128–29n5; and
    funding for Indigenous development,
    education, and environmental preserva-
    tion in Ecuador, 9
United Nations Educational, Scientific and
    Cultural Organization (UNESCO), and
    Intangible Cultural Heritage project, 1,
    2–3, 45, 50, 78–97, 128n1, 129n7
Universidad de las Nacionalidades
    Indígenas de la Amazonía Ecuatoriana
    (UNIDAE), 93
Uquillas, Jorge E., 99, 101, 102, 103, 104
Uzendoski, Michael, 42

Van Cott, Donna Lee, 5, 123
Van den Berg, Maarten H. J., 102–103
Van Nieuwkoop, Marten, 99, 102, 103,
    104
Varese, Stefano, 21
Vargas, Antonio, 118, 129n1
Venezuela, 123
Viatori, Maximilian, 85–88

Waorani (Wao Teredo), 32, 38, 128n6
Warren, Kay B., 14, 27, 121, 126n5
Westwood, Sally, 28
Whitten, Norman E., 24, 127n4
Wilson, Fiona, 58, 69
women: and discourses of Indigeneity and
    environmentalism, 48, 127n2; impact